A Year of Baby Afghans Book 4

Baby gifts are some of my very favorite things to make.
Every special delivery deserves a blanket as soft and sweet as
they are, right? Whether you're looking for spring flowers,
patriotic ripples, an up-to-date granny square, or something
completely different, this collection of 12 crochet baby
afghans is sure to have the perfect match for your little one.
Fun to dream up and fast to finish, baby afghans make great
gifts when shower time arrives, too. Pick your favorite or
work your way through the year…you'll be prepared no
matter when the next shower pops up. And you know that
new mommy will love you for it!

Leisure Arts, Inc.
Maumelle, Arkansas

January

■■□□ EASY

Finished Size: 37¹/₂" x 49¹/₄"
(95.5 cm x 125 cm)

MATERIALS

Medium Weight Yarn [MEDIUM 4]
[3¹/₂ ounces, 201 yards
(100 grams, 184 meters) per skein]:
White - 4 skeins
Lt Blue, Blue, **and** Dk Blue - 3 skeins **each**
Crochet hook, size I (5.5 mm) **or** size needed for
gauge

GAUGE: In pattern, 16 sts = 4¹/₄" (10.75 cm);
24 rows = 6¹/₂" (16.5 cm)

Gauge Swatch: 4¹/₂" x 4¹/₄"
(11.5 cm x 10.75 cm)
With White, ch 18.
Work same as Afghan Body for 16 rows.

Each row is worked across length of Afghan. When
joining yarn and finishing off, leave a 6" (15 cm) end
to be worked into fringe.

STITCH GUIDE

CLUSTER

Ch 3, YO, insert hook in third ch from hook,
YO and pull up a loop, YO and draw through
2 loops on hook, YO, insert hook in **same** ch,
YO and pull up a loop, YO and draw through
2 loops on hook, YO and draw through all
3 loops on hook.

COLOR SEQUENCE

2 Rows **each** of White, ★ Lt Blue, Blue, Dk Blue,
White; repeat from ★ 16 times **more**.

AFGHAN BODY

With White, ch 186, place marker in second ch from
hook for st placement.

Row 1 (Wrong side)**:** Sc in second ch from hook,
(work Cluster, skip next 3 chs, sc in next ch) across;
finish off: 47 sc and 46 Clusters.

Note: Loop a short piece of yarn around **back** of any
stitch on Row 1 to mark **right** side.

Row 2: With **right** side facing, join White with sc
in first sc *(see Joining With Sc, page 45)*; ★ ch 1,
working **behind** next Cluster *(Fig. 2, page 45)*, dc in
second skipped ch **below** Cluster, ch 1, sc in next sc;
repeat from ★ across; finish off: 93 sts and
92 ch-1 sps.

Row 3: With **wrong** side facing, join next color with
sc in first sc; (ch 1, skip next ch-1 sp, sc in next st)
across; finish off.

Row 4: With **right** side facing, join same color with
sc in first sc; (ch 1, sc in next sc) across; finish off.

Row 5: With **wrong** side facing, join next color with
sc in first sc; (ch 1, sc in next sc) across; finish off.

Rows 6-8: Repeat Rows 4 and 5 once, then repeat
Row 4 once **more**.

Row 9: With **wrong** side facing, join White with sc
in first sc; (work Cluster, skip next sc, sc in next sc)
across; finish off: 47 sc and 46 Clusters.

Row 10: With **right** side facing, join White with sc
in first sc; ★ ch 1, working **behind** next Cluster, dc
in skipped sc one row **below** Cluster, ch 1, sc in next
sc; repeat from ★ across; finish off: 93 sts and
92 ch-1 sps.

Rows 11-138: Continuing in Color Sequence,
repeat Rows 3-10, 16 times.

Instructions continued on page 26.

Design by Anne Halliday

February

INTERMEDIATE

Finished Size: 36¹/₂" x 39" (92.5 cm x 99 cm)

MATERIALS

Light Weight Yarn
[1.75 ounces, 170 yards
(50 grams, 155 meters) per skein]: 8 skeins
Crochet hook, size F (3.75 mm) **or** size needed
for gauge
³/₈" (10 mm) wide Satin ribbon - 8 yards
(optional)

Each row of Afghan Body is worked across the length
of the Afghan.

GAUGE: 21 dc = 4" (10 cm); 7 rows = 3" (7.5 cm)

Gauge Swatch: 4" x 3" (10 cm x 7.5 cm)
Ch 23.
Row 1: Dc in fourth ch from hook (**3 skipped chs
count as first dc**) and in each ch across: 21 dc.
Rows 2-7: Ch 3 (**counts as first dc**), turn; dc in next
dc and in each dc across.
Finish off.

STITCH GUIDE

TREBLE CROCHET (*abbreviated tr*)
YO twice, insert hook in stitch indicated, YO
and pull up a loop (4 loops on hook), (YO and
draw through 2 loops on hook) 3 times.
V-STITCH (*abbreviated V-St*)
(Dc, ch 1, dc) in st indicated.
DOUBLE CROCHET DECREASE
   (*abbreviated dc decrease*) (uses next 2 dc)
★ YO, insert hook in **next** dc, YO and pull up
a loop, YO and draw through 2 loops on hook;
repeat from ★ once **more**, YO and draw through
all 3 loops on hook (**counts as one dc**).
PICOT
Ch 3, dc in third ch from hook.

AFGHAN BODY

Ch 187, place marker in third ch from hook for
st placement.

Row 1 (Right side)**:** Dc in fourth ch from hook
(**3 skipped chs count as first dc**) and in each ch
across: 185 dc.

Note: Loop a short piece of yarn around any stitch to
mark Row 1 as **right** side.

Row 2: Ch 3 (**counts as first dc, now and
throughout**), turn; skip next dc, work V-St in next
dc, (skip next 2 dc, work V-St in next dc) across to
last 2 dc, skip next dc, dc in last dc: 61 V-Sts.

Row 3: Ch 4 (**counts as first dc plus ch 1, now and
throughout**), turn; dc decrease, (ch 2, dc decrease)
across to last dc, ch 1, dc in last dc: 63 dc and 62 sps.

Row 4: Ch 3, turn; dc in next ch-1 sp and in next
dc, (2 dc in next ch-2 sp, dc in next dc) across to last
sp, dc in last sp and in last dc: 185 dc.

Row 5: Ch 4, turn; skip next dc, dc in next dc, (ch 1,
skip next dc, dc in next dc) across: 93 dc and
92 ch-1 sps.

Row 6: Ch 4, turn; dc in next dc, (ch 1, dc in next
dc) 3 times, ★ (dc in next ch-1 sp and in next dc) 3
times, (ch 1, dc in next dc) 5 times; repeat from ★
across: 126 dc and 59 ch-1 sps.

Row 7: Ch 4, turn; dc in next dc, (ch 1, dc in next
dc) 3 times, ★ dc in next ch-1 sp and in next 7 dc,
(ch 1, dc in next dc) 4 times; repeat from ★ across:
137 dc and 48 ch-1 sps.

Row 8: Ch 4, turn; dc in next dc, (ch 1, dc in next
dc) 3 times, ★ ch 1, skip next dc, dc in next 7 dc, dc
in next ch-1 sp and in next dc, (ch 1, dc in next dc) 3
times; repeat from ★ across.

Instructions continued on page 26.

Design by Kathryn A. Clark

March

◼◼◼◻ INTERMEDIATE

Finished Size: 39¹/₂" x 45³/₄"
(100.5 cm x 116 cm)

MATERIALS

Light Weight Yarn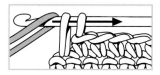
[5 ounces, 455 yards
(140 grams, 416 meters) per skein**]**:
White - 4 skeins
Green - 2 skeins
Yellow - 2 skeins
Crochet hook, size G (4 mm) **or** size needed
for gauge

GAUGE: 16 sts and 24 rows = 4" (10 cm)

Gauge Swatch: 4¹/₄" x 2" (10.75 cm x 5 cm)
Ch 18.
Work same as Afghan Body through Row 12.
Finish off.

STITCH GUIDE

LONG DOUBLE CROCHET
(abbreviated LDC)

YO, working **around** previous rows *(Fig. 2,
page 45)*, insert hook through **both** loops of
specified st, YO and pull up a loop even with
loop on hook, (YO and draw through 2 loops on
hook) twice. Skip st behind LDC.

LONG TREBLE CROCHET *(abbreviated LTR)*

YO twice, working **around** previous rows
(Fig. 2, page 45), insert hook through **both** loops
of specified st, YO and pull up a loop even with
loop on hook (YO and draw through 2 loops on
hook) 3 times. Skip st behind LTR.

FRONT POST DOUBLE CROCHET
(abbreviated FPdc)

YO, insert hook from **front** to **back** around post
of st indicated *(Fig. 5, page 45)*, YO and pull up a
loop (3 loops on hook), (YO and draw through
2 loops on hook) twice.

CHANGING COLORS

Insert hook in stitch indicated, YO and pull up a
loop, drop yarn, with new yarn *(Fig. A)*, YO and
draw through both loops on hook. Do **not** cut old
color until specified in instructions. Carry yarn not
being used loosely along edge.

Fig. A

AFGHAN BODY

With White, ch 154.

Row 1 (Right side)**:** Sc in back ridge of second ch
from hook *(Fig. 3, page 45)* and in each ch across:
153 sc.

Note: Loop a short piece of yarn around any stitch to
mark Row 1 as **right** side.

Row 2: Ch 1, turn; sc in each sc across, changing to
Yellow in last sc.

Row 3: Ch 1, turn; sc in Back Loop Only of first sc
(Fig. 1, page 45), (work LDC in same ch as next sc
on Row 1, sc in Back Loop Only of next sc) across:
76 LDC and 77 sc.

Row 4: Ch 1, turn; sc in **both** loops of first sc and
each st across changing to White in last sc.

Row 5: Ch 1, turn; sc in Back Loop Only of first
2 sc, work LDC in next sc 2 rows **below** next sc, (sc
in Back Loop Only of next sc, work LDC in next sc
2 rows **below** next sc) across to last 2 sc, sc in Back
Loop Only of last 2 sc: 75 LDC and 78 sc.

Instructions continued on page 27

Design by Mary C. Abadir

April

◖▭▭▭▭ EASY

Finished Size: 38" x 51¹/₂" (96.5 cm x 131 cm)

MATERIALS

Medium Weight Yarn ④ MEDIUM
[7 ounces, 364 yards
(198 grams, 333 meters) per skein]:
Blue - 4 skeins
[5 ounces, 244 yards
(141 grams, 223 meters) per skein]:
Variegated - 3 skeins
Crochet hook, size H (5 mm) **or** size needed for gauge
Yarn needle

GAUGE: Each Square = 4¹/₂" (11.5 cm)

Gauge Swatch: 2³/₄" (7 cm) square
Work same as Square through Row 8.

CHANGING COLORS

Insert hook in stitch indicated, YO and pull up a loop, cut old yarn, with new yarn *(Fig. A)*, YO and draw through both loops on hook.

Fig. A

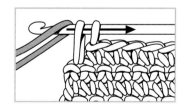

SQUARE (Make 88)

With Variegated, ch 3; join with slip st to form a ring.

Row 1: Ch 1, 3 sc in ring.

Row 2 (Right side): Ch 1, turn; sc in first sc, 3 sc in next sc, sc in last sc: 5 sc.

Note: Loop a short piece of yarn around any stitch to mark Row 2 as **right** side.

Row 3: Ch 1, turn; sc in first 2 sc, 3 sc in next sc, sc in last 2 sc: 7 sc.

Row 4: Ch 1, turn; sc in first 3 sc, 3 sc in next sc, sc in last 3 sc: 9 sc.

Row 5: Ch 1, turn; sc in first 4 sc, 3 sc in next sc, sc in last 4 sc: 11 sc.

Row 6: Ch 1, turn; sc in first 5 sc, 3 sc in next sc, sc in last 5 sc: 13 sc.

Row 7: Ch 1, turn; sc in first 6 sc, 3 sc in next sc, sc in last 6 sc: 15 sc.

Row 8: Ch 1, turn; sc in first 7 sc, 3 sc in next sc, sc in last 7 sc changing to Blue in last sc: 17 sc.

Row 9: Ch 4 (**counts as first dc plus ch 1, now and throughout**), turn; (skip next sc, dc in next sc, ch 1) 3 times, skip next sc, (dc, ch 3, dc) in next sc, (ch 1, skip next sc, dc in next sc) 4 times: 10 dc and 9 sps.

Row 10: Ch 1, turn; sc in first dc, (sc in next ch-1 sp and in next dc) 4 times, 5 sc in next ch-3 sp, sc in next dc, (sc in next ch-1 sp and in next dc) 4 times: 23 sc.

Row 11: Ch 4, turn; (skip next sc, dc in next sc, ch 1) 5 times, (dc, ch 3, dc) in next sc, ch 1, dc in next sc, (ch 1, skip next sc, dc in next sc) 5 times; do **not** finish off: 14 dc and 13 sps.

Instructions continued on page 29.

Design by Bonita Dubil

May

▰▰▰▱ INTERMEDIATE

Finished Size: 27" x 36" (68.5 cm x 91.5 cm)

MATERIALS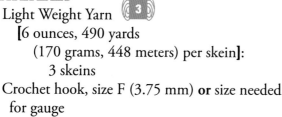

Light Weight Yarn
[6 ounces, 490 yards
(170 grams, 448 meters) per skein]:
3 skeins
Crochet hook, size F (3.75 mm) **or** size needed
for gauge

GAUGE SWATCH: 2¹/₂" (6.25 cm) square
Work same as First Square.

STITCH GUIDE
TREBLE CROCHET (*abbreviated tr*)
YO twice, insert hook in sp indicated, YO and
pull up a loop (4 loops on hook), (YO and
draw through 2 loops on hook) 3 times.

The method used to connect the pieces is a no-sew
joining also known as "join-as-you-go." After
the First Square is made, each remaining piece is
worked to the last round, then crocheted together
as the last round is worked. Holding pieces with
wrong sides together, work single crochet into
stitch or space as indicated (*Fig. A*).

Fig. A

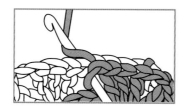

FIRST STRIP
FIRST SQUARE
Ch 5; join with slip st to form a ring.

Push tr to **right** side.

Rnd 1 (Wrong side)**:** Ch 1, (sc, tr) 8 times in ring;
join with slip st to first sc: 16 sts.

Note: Loop a short piece of yarn around **back** of
any stitch on Rnd 1 to mark **right** side.

Rnd 2: Ch 1, turn; sc in same st, (ch 3, skip next
tr, sc in next sc) around to last tr, skip last tr, dc in
first sc to form last ch-3 sp: 8 ch-3 sps.

Rnd 3: Ch 1, turn; (sc, tr, sc) in last ch-3 sp made,
(sc, ch 3, sc) in next ch-3 sp, ★ (sc, tr, sc, ch 3, sc,
tr, sc) in next ch-3 sp, (sc, ch 3, sc) in next ch-3 sp;
repeat from ★ around, (sc, tr, sc) in same sp as first
sc, dc in first sc to form last ch-3 sp: 24 sc and
8 ch-3 sps.

Rnd 4: Ch 1, turn; sc in last ch-3 sp made, ★ † ch 3,
skip next tr, sc in next sc, (sc, ch 3, sc) in next ch-3 sp,
skip next sc, sc in next sc, ch 3 †, (sc, ch 3, sc) in next
ch-3 sp; repeat from ★ 2 times **more**, then repeat from
† to † once, sc in same sp as first sc, ch 3; join with
slip st to first sc, finish off: 16 ch-3 sps.

ADDITIONAL 13 SQUARES
Work same as First Square through Rnd 3: 24 sc
and 8 ch-3 sps.

Instructions continued on page 29.

11

Design by Katherine Satterfield

June

Finished Size: 34" (86.5 cm) square

MATERIALS

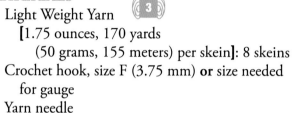

Light Weight Yarn
  [1.75 ounces, 170 yards
    (50 grams, 155 meters) per skein]: 8 skeins
Crochet hook, size F (3.75 mm) **or** size needed
    for gauge
Yarn needle

GAUGE SWATCH: 3³/₄" (9.5 cm) square
Work same as Square A.

STITCH GUIDE

REVERSE SINGLE CROCHET
(abbreviated reverse sc)

Working from left to **right**, ★ insert hook in st
to **right** of hook *(Fig. A)*, YO and draw through,
under and to left of loop on hook (2 loops on
hook) *(Fig. B)*, YO and draw through both
loops on hook *(Fig. C)* (**reverse sc made,**
Fig. D); repeat from ★ around.

Fig. A

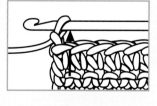

Fig. B

Fig. C

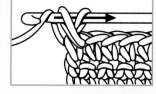

Fig. D

SQUARE A (Make 41)

Ch 5; join with slip st to form a ring.

Rnd 1 (Right side)**:** Ch 1, (3 sc in ring, ch 2) 4 times;
join with slip st to first sc: 12 sc and 4 ch-2 sps.

Note: Loop a short piece of yarn around any stitch
to mark Rnd 1 as **right** side.

Rnd 2: Ch 2 (**counts as first hdc, now and
throughout**), hdc in next 2 sc, (2 hdc, ch 2, hdc) in
next ch-2 sp, ★ hdc in next 3 sc, (2 hdc, ch 2, hdc)
in next ch-2 sp; repeat from ★ 2 times **more**; join
with slip st to first hdc: 24 hdc and 4 ch-2 sps.

Rnd 3: Ch 1, sc in same st and in next 4 hdc, (2 sc,
ch 2, sc) in next ch-2 sp, ★ sc in next 6 hdc, (2 sc,
ch 2, sc) in next ch-2 sp; repeat from ★ 2 times
more, sc in last hdc; join with slip st to first sc: 36 sc
and 4 ch-2 sps.

Rnd 4: Ch 2, hdc in next 6 sc, (2 hdc, ch 2, hdc) in
next ch-2 sp, ★ hdc in next 9 sc, (2 hdc, ch 2, hdc)
in next ch-2 sp; repeat from ★ 2 times **more**, hdc in
last 2 sc; join with slip st to first hdc: 48 hdc and
4 ch-2 sps.

Rnd 5: Ch 1, sc in same st and in next 8 hdc,
(2 sc, ch 2, sc) in next ch-2 sp, ★ sc in next 12 hdc,
(2 sc, ch 2, sc) in next ch-2 sp; repeat from ★ 2 times **more**,
sc in last 3 hdc; join with slip st to first hdc: 60 sc
and 4 ch-2 sps.

Rnd 6: Ch 2, hdc in next 10 sc, (2 hdc, ch 2, hdc)
in next ch-2 sp, ★ hdc in next 15 sc, (2 hdc, ch 2,
hdc) in next ch-2 sp; repeat from ★ 2 times **more**,
hdc in last 4 sc; join with slip st to first hdc,
finish off: 72 hdc and 4 ch-2 sps.

Instructions continued on page 30.

13

Design by Kathryn A. Clark

July

Finished Size: 32" x 45¹/₂" (81.5 cm x 115.5 cm)

MATERIALS

Light Weight Yarn 🧶 **LIGHT 3**
[2¹/₂ ounces, 168 yards
(70 grams, 154 meters) per skein]:
White - 11 skeins
Blue - 5 skeins
Red - 1 skein
Crochet hook, size F (3.75 mm) **or** size needed
for gauge

GAUGE: In pattern, one point to point
repeat (25 sts) = 3¹/₂" (9 cm);
Rows 1-8 = 2¹/₂" (6.25 cm)

Gauge Swatch: 7¹/₄"w x 4¹/₄"h
(18.5 cm x 10.75 cm)
With White, ch 49.
Work same as Afghan Body for 14 rows.
Finish off.

STITCH GUIDE

BOBBLE (uses one st or sp)
★ YO, insert hook in st or sp indicated, YO
and pull up a loop, YO and draw through
2 loops on hook; repeat from ★ 4 times **more**,
YO and draw through all 6 loops on hook.

CHANGING COLORS

Insert hook in stitch indicated, YO and pull up a
loop, cut old yarn, with new yarn *(Fig. A)*, YO and
draw through both loops on hook.

Fig. A

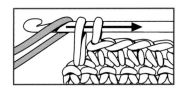

AFGHAN BODY

With White, ch 224.

Row 1 (Right side)**:** Sc in second ch from hook and
in next 10 chs, 3 sc in next ch, sc in next 11 chs,
★ skip next 2 chs, sc in next 11 chs, 3 sc in next ch,
sc in next 11 chs; repeat from ★ across: 225 sc.

Note: Loop a short piece of yarn around any stitch
to mark Row 1 as **right** side.

Always leave last sc unworked at end of each row.

Row 2: Ch 1, turn; skip first sc, ★ † sc in next sc,
(ch 1, skip next sc, sc in next sc) 5 times, 3 sc in
next sc, sc in next sc, (ch 1, skip next sc, sc in next
sc) 5 times †, skip next 2 sc; repeat from ★ 7 times
more, then repeat from † to † once: 135 sc and
90 ch-1 sps.

Rows 3-7: Ch 1, turn; ★ (sc in next ch-1 sp, ch 1)
5 times, skip next sc, sc in next sc, 3 sc in next sc, sc
in next sc, (ch 1, sc in next ch-1 sp) 5 times; repeat
from ★ across.

Row 8: Ch 1, turn; ★ (sc in next ch-1 sp, ch 1) 5
times, skip next sc, sc in next sc, 3 sc in next sc, sc
in next sc, (ch 1, sc in next ch-1 sp) 5 times; repeat
from ★ across, changing to Blue in last sc.

Row 9: Ch 1, turn; ★ † sc in next ch-1 sp and in
next sc, work Bobble in next ch-1 sp, sc in next sc
and in next ch-1 sp, work Bobble in next sc, sc in
next ch-1 sp and in next sc, work Bobble in next
ch-1 sp, sc in next 2 sc, (sc, work Bobble, sc) in next
sc, sc in next 2 sc, work Bobble in next ch-1 sp, sc
in next sc and in next ch-1 sp, work Bobble in next
sc, sc in next ch-1 sp and in next sc, work Bobble
in next ch-1 sp, sc in next sc and in next ch-1 sp †,
skip next 2 sc; repeat from ★ 7 times **more**, then
repeat from † to † once, changing to White in last
sc: 63 Bobbles and 162 sc.

Instructions continued on page 32.

Design by Becky Stevens

August

▣▣▣▣▢ EXPERIENCED

Finished Size: 37" (94 cm) square

MATERIALS

Medium Weight Yarn
[3¹/₂ ounces, 150 yards
(100 grams, 137 meters) per skein]: 7 skeins
Crochet hook, size J (6 mm) **or** size needed for
gauge

GAUGE: 16 sc and 16 rows = 4" (10 cm)

Gauge Swatch: 4" (10 cm) square
Ch 17.
Row 1: Sc in second ch from hook and in each ch
across: 16 sc.
Rows 2-16: Ch 1, turn; sc in each sc across.
Finish off.

STITCH GUIDE

FRONT POST DOUBLE CROCHET
(abbreviated FPdc)
YO, insert hook from **front** to **back** around post
of st indicated *(Fig. 5, page 45)*, YO and pull
up a loop (3 loops on hook), (YO and draw
through 2 loops on hook) twice. Skip st behind
FPdc.

AFGHAN BODY

Ch 4; join with slip st to form a ring.

Rnd 1 (Right side): Ch 3, 2 dc in ring, (ch 1, 3 dc in
ring) 3 times, sc in third ch of beginning ch to form
last ch-1 sp: 12 sts and 4 ch-1 sps.

Note: Loop a short piece of yarn around any stitch to
mark Rnd 1 as **right** side.

Rnd 2: Ch 2 (**counts as first hdc, now and
throughout**); work FPdc around next 3 sts, ★ (hdc,
ch 1, hdc) in next ch-1 sp, work FPdc around next
3 dc; repeat from ★ 2 times **more**, hdc in same sp as
first hdc, sc in first hdc to form last ch-1 sp: 20 sts
and 4 ch-1 sps.

Be careful to work into or around the first hdc
(beginning ch-2) on each of the following rnds.

Rnd 3: Ch 2, work FPdc around each of next
5 sts, ★ (hdc, ch 1, hdc) in next ch-1 sp, work FPdc
around each of next 5 sts; repeat from ★ 2 times
more, hdc in same sp as first hdc, sc in first hdc to
form last ch-1 sp: 28 sts and 4 ch-1 sps.

Rnd 4: Ch 2, work FPdc around each of next
7 sts, ★ (hdc, ch 1, hdc) in next ch-1 sp, work FPdc
around each of next 7 sts; repeat from ★ 2 times
more, hdc in same sp as first hdc, sc in first hdc to
form last ch-1 sp: 36 sts and 4 ch-1 sps.

Rnd 5: Ch 2, sc in Back Loop Only of next 9 sts
(Fig. 1, page 45), ★ (hdc, ch 1, hdc) in next ch-1 sp,
sc in Back Loop Only of next 9 sts; repeat from ★
2 times **more**, hdc in same sp as first hdc, sc in first
hdc to form last ch-1 sp: 44 sts and 4 ch-1 sps.

Rnd 6: Ch 2, ★ † work FPdc around next hdc, sc
in Back Loop Only of next 9 sc, work FPdc around
next hdc †, (hdc, ch 1, hdc) in next ch-1 sp; repeat
from ★ 2 times **more**, then repeat from † to † once,
hdc in same sp as first hdc, sc in first hdc to form
last ch-1 sp: 52 sts and 4 ch-1 sps.

Rnd 7: Ch 2, ★ † work FPdc around each of next
2 sts, sc in Back Loop Only of next 9 sc, work FPdc
around each of next 2 sts †, (hdc, ch 1, hdc) in next
ch-1 sp; repeat from ★ 2 times **more**, then repeat
from † to † once, hdc in same sp as first hdc, sc in
first hdc to form last ch-1 sp: 60 sts and 4 ch-1 sps.

Instructions continued on page 33.

17

Design by C. A. Riley

September

Finished Size: 38" x 47" (96.5 cm x 119.5 cm)

MATERIALS

LIGHT 3

Light Weight Yarn
[3¹/₂ ounces, 257 yards
(100 grams, 235 meters) per skein]:
White - 3 skeins
Blue - 2 skeins
Pink, Green, Orange, Yellow, **and**
Lavender - 1 skein **each**
Crochet hook, size E (3.5 mm) **or** size needed
for gauge
Yarn needle

GAUGE SWATCH: 3" (7.5 cm) square
Work same as Square.

SQUARE (Make 180 total)

Note: Referring to table below for color sequence,
make 15 **each** of Squares 1-12.

Square	Rnd 1	Rnds 2 & 3	Rnd 4	Rnd 5
1	Orange	Green	Blue	White
2	Blue	White	Orange	Green
3	Pink	Blue	White	Lavender
4	Lavender	Blue	Pink	White
5	Green	White	Lavender	Orange
6	White	Pink	Blue	Yellow
7	Green	Pink	Yellow	White
8	Orange	Yellow	White	Blue
9	Pink	Yellow	White	Lavender
10	White	Green	Yellow	Orange
11	Blue	Lavender	Orange	White
12	Yellow	White	Blue	Pink

With first color, ch 4; join with slip st to form
a ring.

Rnd 1 (Right side)**:** Ch 3 (**counts as first hdc plus
ch 1**), (hdc in ring, ch 1) 7 times; join with slip st to
first hdc, finish off: 8 ch-1 sps.

Note: Loop a short piece of yarn around any stitch to
mark Rnd 1 as **right** side.

Rnd 2: With **right** side facing, join next color with
slip st in any ch-1 sp; ch 1, sc in same sp, ch 3, (sc in
next ch-1 sp, ch 3) around; join with slip st to first sc.

Rnd 3: (Slip st, ch 1, 4 sc) in first ch-3 sp, place
marker around second sc made for stitch placement,
4 sc in next ch-3 sp and in each ch-3 sp around; join
with slip st to first sc, finish off: 32 sc.

Rnd 4: With **right** side facing, join next color with
slip st in marked sc, remove marker; ch 3 (**counts as
first dc, now and throughout**), dc in same st, 2 dc in
next sc, ch 1, skip next 2 sc, 2 dc in each of next
2 sc, ch 3, skip next 2 sc, ★ 2 dc in each of next 2 sc,
ch 1, skip next 2 sc, 2 dc in each of next 2 sc, ch 3,
skip next 2 sc; repeat from ★ around; join with slip st
to first dc, finish off: 32 dc and 8 sps.

Rnd 5: With **right** side facing, join next color with
slip st in any ch-3 sp; ch 3, (2 dc, ch 1, 3 dc) in same
sp, hdc in next 3 dc, skip next dc, dc in next ch-1 sp,
skip next dc, hdc in next 3 dc, ★ (3 dc, ch 1, 3 dc)
in next ch-3 sp, hdc in next 3 dc, skip next dc, dc in
next ch-1 sp, skip next dc, hdc in next 3 dc; repeat
from ★ around; join with slip st to first dc, finish off.

ASSEMBLY

With corresponding color yarn, using Placement
Diagram as a guide (page 42), and working through
inside loops only, whipstitch Squares together forming
12 vertical strips of 15 Squares each *(Fig. 7a, page 46)*,
beginning in first corner ch-1 and ending in next
corner ch-1; then whipstitch strips together in same
manner.

Instructions continued on page 42.

Design by Jennine Korejko

October

⬛⬛◻◻◻ EASY

Finished Size: 34¹/₄" x 45" (87 cm x 114.5 cm)

MATERIALS

Light Weight Yarn LIGHT 3
 [1³/₄ ounces, 133 yards
  (50 grams, 122 meters) per skein]:
   White - 9 skeins
   Pink - 7 skeins
Crochet hook, size G (4 mm) **or** size needed
 for gauge

GAUGE: In pattern,
     13 sts and 12 rows = 3¹/₄" (8.25 cm)

Gauge Swatch: 7" x 2¹/₂" (17.75 cm x 6.25 cm)
Ch 29.
Work same as Afghan Body for 9 rows.
Finish off.

Each row is worked across length of Afghan. When joining yarn and finishing off, leave a 7" (18 cm) end to be worked into fringe.

STITCH GUIDE
DOUBLE TREBLE CROCHET
  (abbreviated dtr)
YO 3 times, insert hook in sc indicated, YO and pull up a loop (5 loops on hook), (YO and draw through 2 loops on hook) 4 times.

AFGHAN BODY
With Pink, ch 181.

Row 1 (Wrong side): Sc in second ch from hook and in each ch across; finish off: 180 sc.

Note: Loop a short piece of yarn around **back** of any stitch on Row 1 to mark **right** side.

Row 2: With **right** side facing, join White with sc in first sc *(see Joining With Sc, page 45)*; sc in next 3 sc, ★ ch 1, skip next sc, sc in next 2 sc, ch 1, skip next sc, sc in next 4 sc; repeat from ★ across; finish off: 136 sc and 44 ch-1 sps.

Row 3: With **wrong** side facing, join White with dc in first sc *(see Joining With Dc, page 45)*; dc in next sc and in each sc and each ch-1 sp across; finish off: 180 dc.

Row 4: With **right** side facing, join Pink with sc in first dc; sc in next 3 dc, working in **front** of previous rows, dtr in second skipped sc 3 rows **below**, skip dc **behind** dtr on previous row, sc in next 2 dc, working in **front** of last dtr made, dtr in first skipped sc 3 rows **below**, skip dc **behind** dtr on previous row, sc in next 4 dc, ★ skip next skipped sc 3 rows **below**, working in **front** of previous rows, dtr in next skipped sc, skip dc **behind** dtr on previous row, sc in next 2 dc, working in **front** of last dtr made, dtr in skipped sc 3 rows **below**, skip dc **behind** dtr on previous row, sc in next 4 dc; repeat from ★ across; finish off: 136 sc and 44 dtr.

Row 5: With **wrong** side facing, join Pink with sc in first sc; sc in next sc and in each st across; finish off: 180 sc.

Row 6: With **right** side facing, join White with sc in first sc; sc in next 7 sc, ch 1, skip next sc, sc in next 2 sc, ch 1, ★ skip next sc, sc in next 4 sc, ch 1, skip next sc, sc in next 2 sc, ch 1; repeat from ★ across to last 9 sc, skip next sc, sc in last 8 sc; finish off: 138 sc and 42 ch-1 sps.

Row 7: With **wrong** side facing, join White with dc in first sc; dc in next sc and in each sc and each ch-1 sp across; finish off: 180 dc.

Instructions continued on page 42.

Design by Kay Meadors

November

Finished Size: 38½" x 47½" (98 cm x 120.5 cm)

MATERIALS

Medium Weight Yarn ④

[3½ ounces, 207 yards
(100 grams, 188 meters) per skein]:
Ecru - 4 skeins
Brown - 2 skeins
Gold - 2 skeins
Crochet hooks, sizes I (5.5 mm) **and** J (6 mm) **or**
sizes needed for gauge

GAUGE: With larger size hook, in pattern,
11 sts and 6 rows = 4" (10 cm)

Gauge Swatch: 4" (10 cm) square.
With larger size hook, ch 16.
Work same as Afghan Body for 6 rows.

STITCH GUIDE

LONG DOUBLE CROCHET
(abbreviated LDC)
YO, working **around** previous rows *(Fig. 2, page 45)*, insert hook in sp indicated, YO and pull up a loop even with last st made (3 loops on hook), (YO and draw through 2 loops on hook) twice.

CHANGING COLORS

YO, insert hook in stitch indicated, YO and pull up a loop, YO and draw through 2 loops on hook, cut old yarn, with new yarn *(Fig. A)*, YO and draw through 2 loops on hook.

Fig. A

AFGHAN BODY

With larger size hook and Brown, ch 132, place marker in third ch from hook for st placement.

Row 1 (Right side)**:** Dc in fourth ch from hook (**3 skipped chs count as first dc**), (ch 1, skip next 2 chs, dc in next 2 chs) across: 66 dc and 32 ch-1 sps.

Note: Loop a short piece of yarn around any stitch to mark Row 1 as **right** side.

Row 2: Ch 3 (**counts as first dc, now and throughout**), turn; dc in sp **before** next dc *(Fig. 6b, page 46)*, ch 1, (skip next 2 dc, 2 dc in sp **before** next dc, ch 1) across to last 3 dc, skip next 2 dc, dc in sp **before** next dc, dc in last dc changing to Ecru.

Row 3: Ch 3, turn; dc in sp **before** next dc, skip next dc, work LDC in ch-1 sp 2 rows **below**, ★ skip next dc, 2 dc in sp **before** next dc, skip next dc, work LDC in ch-1 sp 2 rows **below**; repeat from ★ across to last 2 dc, skip next dc, dc in sp **before** next dc, dc in last dc, finish off: 66 dc and 32 LDC.

Row 4: With **right** side facing, join Gold with slip st in first dc, ch 3; dc in sp **before** next dc, ch 1, (skip next 3 sts, 2 dc in sp **before** next dc, ch 1) across to last 4 sts, skip next 3 sts, dc in sp **before** next dc, dc in last dc: 66 dc and 32 ch-1 sps.

Row 5: Ch 3, turn; dc in sp **before** next dc, ch 1, (skip next 2 dc, 2 dc in sp **before** next dc, ch 1) across to last 3 dc, skip next 2 dc, dc in sp **before** next dc, dc in last dc changing to Ecru.

Row 6: Ch 3, turn; dc in sp **before** next dc, skip next dc, work LDC in ch-1 sp 2 rows **below**, ★ skip next dc, 2 dc in sp **before** next dc, skip next dc, work LDC in ch-1 sp 2 rows **below**; repeat from ★ across to last 2 dc, skip next dc, dc in sp **before** next dc, dc in last dc, finish off: 66 dc and 32 LDC.

Instructions continued on page 43.

Design by Martha Brooks Stein

December

Finished Size: 33¼" x 50½"
(84.5 cm x 128.5 cm)

MATERIALS
Medium Weight Yarn
[3 ounces, 160 yards
(85 grams, 146 meters) per skein]: 8 skeins
Crochet hook, size H (5 mm) **or** size needed
for gauge
³/₈" (10 mm) Ribbon - 6 yards (optional)

GAUGE: In pattern, 3 repeats = 5" (12.75 cm);
8 rows = 4" (10 cm)

Gauge Swatch: 5" x 4" (12.75 cm x 10 cm)
Ch 20.
Work same as Afghan Body through Row 8.
Finish off.

AFGHAN BODY
Ch 104.

Row 1: Sc in second ch from hook and in each ch
across: 103 sc.

Row 2 (Right side): Ch 1, turn; sc in first sc, ★ skip
next 2 sc, 5 dc in next sc, skip next 2 sc, sc in next
sc; repeat from ★ across: 85 dc and 18 sc.

Note: Loop a short piece of yarn around any stitch
to mark Row 2 as **right** side.

Row 3: Ch 3 (**counts as first dc, now and
throughout**), turn; 2 dc in same st, skip next 2 dc, sc
in next dc, (5 dc in next sc, skip next 2 dc, sc in next
dc) across to last 3 sts, skip next 2 dc, 3 dc in last sc:
86 dc and 17 sc.

Row 4: Ch 1, turn; sc in first dc, (5 dc in next sc,
skip next 2 dc, sc in next dc) across: 85 dc and 18 sc.

Rows 5-91: Repeat Rows 3 and 4, 43 times; then
repeat Row 3 once **more**.

Do **not** finish off.

BORDER
Row 1: Ch 1, do **not** turn; working in end of rows,
work 155 sc evenly spaced across; working in free
loops of beginning ch *(Fig. 4b, page 45)*, 3 sc in first
ch, work 99 sc evenly spaced across to last ch, 3 sc in
last ch; working in end of rows, work 155 sc evenly
spaced across: 415 sc.

Row 2: Ch 1, turn; sc in first sc, ★ skip next 2 sc,
5 dc in next sc, skip next 2 sc, sc in next sc; repeat
from ★ across, do **not** finish off: 345 dc and 70 sc.

EDGING
Rnd 1 (Eyelet rnd)**:** Ch 5 (**counts as first dc plus
ch 2**), do **not** turn; dc in same st, ch 2; working
across sts on Row 91 of Afghan Body, sc in first dc,
ch 2, (dc in next sc, ch 2, skip next 2 dc, sc in next
dc, ch 2) across to last 3 dc, skip last 3 dc; working
across sts on Row 2 of Border, (dc, ch 2) twice in
first sc, † skip next 2 dc, sc in next dc, ch 2, (dc in
next sc, ch 2, skip next 2 dc, sc in next dc, ch 2)
25 times †, (dc, ch 2) twice in next sc, skip next
2 dc, sc in next dc, ch 2, (dc in next sc, ch 2, skip
next 2 dc, sc in next dc, ch 2) 16 times, (dc, ch 2)
twice in next sc, repeat from † to † once; join with
slip st to first dc: 176 ch-2 sps.

Rnd 2: Slip st in first ch-2 sp, ch 1, sc in same sp,
ch 5, ★ (sc in next ch-2 sp, ch 5) across to next
corner ch-2 sp, (sc, ch 5) twice in corner ch-2 sp;
repeat from ★ 2 times **more**, (sc in next ch-2 sp,
ch 5) across, sc in same sp as first sc, ch 2, dc in first
sc to form last ch-5 sp: 180 ch-5 sps.

Instructions continued on page 43.

Design by Ginger Thomas

January
(continued from page 2)

TRIM
FIRST SIDE
With **right** side facing, join White with slip st in first sc on Row 138; slip st in next ch-1 sp, (ch 1, slip st in next ch-1 sp) across to last sc, slip st in last sc; finish off.

SECOND SIDE
With **right** side facing and working in sps and in free loops of beginning ch *(Fig. 4b, page 45)*, join White with slip st in marked ch; slip st in next sp, (ch 1, slip st in next sp) across to last ch, slip st in last ch; finish off.

Holding two 13" (33 cm) strands of corresponding color yarn together, add fringe in end of each row across short edges of Afghan *(Figs. 8a & b, page 46)*.

February
(continued from page 4)

Row 9: Ch 4, turn; dc in next dc, (ch 1, dc in next dc) twice, ★ † ch 1, skip next dc, dc in next 7 dc, dc in next ch-1 sp and in next dc †, (ch 1, dc in next dc) 3 times; repeat from ★ 9 times **more**, then repeat from † to † once, (ch 1, dc in next dc) 4 times.

Row 10: Ch 4, turn; dc in next dc, (ch 1, dc in next dc) twice, ★ † ch 1, dc in next 7 dc, ch 1, skip next dc, dc in next dc †, (ch 1, dc in next dc) 3 times; repeat from ★ 9 times **more**, then repeat from † to † once, (ch 1, dc in next dc) 4 times: 126 dc and 59 ch-1 sps.

Row 11: Ch 4, turn; dc in next dc, (ch 1, dc in next dc) 4 times, (ch 1, skip next dc, dc in next dc) 3 times, ★ (ch 1, dc in next dc) 5 times, (ch 1, skip next dc, dc in next dc) 3 times; repeat from ★ 9 times **more**, (ch 1, dc in next dc) 4 times: 93 dc and 92 ch-1 sps.

Row 12: Ch 3, turn; dc in first ch-1 sp and in each ch-1 sp and each dc across: 185 dc.

Rows 13-16: Repeat Rows 2-5.

Row 17: Ch 3, turn; dc in first ch-1 sp and in each ch-1 sp and each dc across: 185 dc.

Rows 18-79: Repeat Rows 2-17, 3 times; then repeat Rows 2-15 once **more**; at end of Row 79, do **not** finish off.

EDGING
Note: When working twice into the end of same row, work in top of dc **and** around dc.

Rnd 1 (Eyelet rnd)**:** Ch 5 (**counts as first tr plus ch 1, now and throughout**), do **not** turn; dc in top of last dc on Row 79, ch 1, working in end of rows, ★ † (dc in next row, ch 1) twice, (dc, ch 1) twice in next row; repeat from ★ across to last 3 rows †, (dc in next row, ch 1) 3 times; working in free loops of beginning ch *(Fig. 4b, page 45)*, (dc, ch 1, tr, ch 1, dc) in first ch, ch 1, skip next ch, (dc in next ch, ch 1, skip next ch) across to marked ch, (dc, ch 1, tr, ch 1, dc) in marked ch, ch 1; working in end of rows, repeat from † to † once, (dc in next row, ch 1) twice; working across Row 79, (dc, ch 1, tr, ch 1, dc) in first dc, ch 1, skip next dc, (dc in next dc, ch 1, skip next dc) across, dc in same st as first tr, ch 1; join with slip st to first tr: 400 ch-1 sps.

Rnd 2: Ch 5, dc in same st, ch 1, ★ (dc in next dc, ch 1) across to next tr, (dc, ch 1, tr, ch 1, dc) in next tr, ch 1; repeat from ★ 2 times **more**, (dc in next dc, ch 1) across, dc in same st as first tr, ch 1; join with slip st to first tr: 408 ch-1 sps.

Rnd 3: Ch 1, sc in same st, ch 1, skip next ch-1 sp, (dc, work Picot, dc) in next ch-1 sp, ch 1, ★ skip next dc and next ch-1 sp, sc in next st, ch 1, skip next ch-1 sp, (dc, work Picot, dc) in next ch-1 sp, ch 1; repeat from ★ around; join with slip st to first sc, finish off.

Optional: Divide ribbon into four equal lengths. With **right** side facing and beginning at any corner, weave one length of ribbon through sps of Eyelet rnd on one edge of Afghan Body. Repeat for remaining edges. Tie ends of ribbon in a bow at each corner and tack bows to secure. Trim ends as desired.

March

(continued from page 6)

Row 6: Ch 1, turn; sc in **both** loops of first sc and each st across changing to Yellow in last sc.

Row 7: Ch 1, turn; sc in Back Loop Only of first sc, (work LDC in next sc 2 rows **below** next sc, sc in Back Loop Only of next sc) across: 76 LDC and 77 sc.

Rows 8-10: Repeat Rows 4-6; at end of Row 10, cut White.

Row 11: Ch 1, turn; sc in Back Loop Only of first sc, (work LDC in next sc 2 rows **below** next sc, sc in Back Loop Only of next sc) across changing to White in last sc; cut Yellow: 76 LDC and 77 sc.

Row 12: Ch 1, turn; sc in **both** loops of first sc and each st across, changing to Green in last sc; cut White.

Row 13: Ch 1, turn; sc in first 3 sc, work LDC in fifth sc 3 rows **below** next sc, sc in next sc, work LDC in same sc as previous LDC, ★ sc in next 5 sc, skip next 7 sc on same row as last LDC worked, work LDC in next sc, sc in next sc, work LDC in same sc as previous LDC; repeat from ★ across to last 3 sc, sc in last 3 sc changing to White in last sc: 38 LDC and 115 sc.

Row 14: Ch 1, turn; sc in first sc and in each st across, changing to Green in last sc; cut White.

Row 15: Ch 1, turn; sc in first 2 sc, work FPdc around next LDC, skip sc behind FPdc, sc in next sc, work LTR in same st as LDC, sc in next sc, work FPdc around next LDC, ★ skip sc behind FPdc, sc in next 3 sc, work FPdc around next LDC, skip sc behind FPdc, sc in next sc, work LTR in same st as LDC, sc in next sc, work FPdc around next LDC; repeat from ★ across to last 3 sc, skip sc behind FPdc, sc in last 2 sc changing to White in last sc; cut Green: 38 FPdc, 19 LTR, and 96 sc.

Row 16: Ch 1, turn; sc in first sc and in each st across changing to Yellow in last sc; cut White.

Row 17: Ch 1, turn; sc in first 4 sc, work 3 FPdc around next LTR, (skip sc behind FPdc, sc in next 7 sc, work 3 FPdc around next LTR) across to last 5 sc, skip sc behind FPdc, sc in last 4 sc changing to White in last sc; cut Yellow: 19 3-FPdc groups and 134 sc.

Row 18: Ch 1, turn; sc in first 4 sc, working in **front** of next 3-FPdc group, dc in skipped sc, skip 3 FPdc, ★ sc in next 7 sc, working in **front** of next 3-FPdc group, dc in skipped sc, skip 3 FPdc; repeat from ★ across to last 4 sc, sc in last 4 sc: 153 sts.

Row 19: Ch 1, turn; sc in Back Loop Only of first sc and each st across.

Row 20: Ch 1, turn; sc in **both** loops of first sc and each sc across changing to Green in last sc.

Row 21: Ch 1, turn; sc in Back Loop Only of first sc, (work LDC in next sc 2 rows **below** next sc, sc in Back Loop Only of next sc) across: 76 LDC and 77 sc.

Row 22: Ch 1, turn; sc in **both** loops of first sc and each st across changing to White in last sc.

Row 23: Ch 1, turn; sc in Back Loop Only of first 2 sc, work LDC in next sc 2 rows **below** next sc, (sc in Back Loop Only of next sc, work LDC in next sc 2 rows **below** next sc) across to last 2 sc, sc in Back Loop Only of last 2 sc: 75 LDC and 78 sc.

Instructions continued on page 28.

Row 24: Ch 1, turn; sc in **both** loops of first sc and each st across changing to Green in last st.

Rows 25-28: Repeat Rows 21-24; at end of Row 28, cut White.

Row 29: Ch 1, turn; sc in Back Loop Only of first sc, (work LDC in next sc 2 rows **below** next sc, sc in Back Loop Only of next sc) across changing to White in last sc; cut Green: 76 LDC and 77 sc.

Row 30: Ch 1, turn; sc in **both** loops of first sc and each st across.

Row 31: Ch 1, turn; sc in Back Loop Only of first 2 sc, work LDC in next sc 2 rows **below** next sc, (sc in Back Loop Only of next sc, work LDC in next sc 2 rows **below** next sc) across to last 2 sc, sc in Back Loop Only of last 2 sc: 75 LDC and 78 sc.

Row 32: Ch 1, turn; sc in **both** loops of first sc and each st across.

Row 33: Ch 1, turn; sc in Back Loop Only of first sc, (work LDC in next sc 2 rows **below** next sc, sc in Back Loop Only of next sc) across: 76 LDC and 77 sc.

Row 34: Ch 1, turn; sc in **both** loops of first sc and each st across.

Row 35: Ch 1, turn; sc in Back Loop Only of first 2 sc, work LDC in next sc 2 rows **below** next sc, (sc in Back Loop Only of next sc, work LDC in next sc 2 rows **below**) across to last 2 sc, sc in Back Loop Only of last 2 sc: 75 LDC and 78 sc.

Row 36: Ch 1, turn; sc in **both** loops of first sc and each st across changing to Yellow in last sc.

Row 37: Ch 1, turn; sc in Back Loop Only of first sc, (work LDC in next sc 2 rows **below** next sc, sc in Back Loop Only of next sc) across: 76 LDC and 77 sc.

Rows 38-265: Repeat Rows 4-37, 6 times; then repeat Rows 4-27 once **more**.

Row 266: Ch 1, turn; sc in **both** loops of first sc and each st across changing to Green in last st; cut White.

EDGING

Rnd 1: Ch 1, turn; 3 sc in Back Loop Only of first sc, LDC in next sc 2 rows **below** next sc, (sc in Back Loop Only of next sc, LDC in next sc 2 rows **below** next sc) across to last sc, 3 sc in Back Loop Only of last sc; sc evenly across end of rows; working in free loops of beginning ch *(Fig. 4b, page 45)*, 3 sc in first ch, sc in each ch across to last ch, 3 sc in last ch; sc evenly across end of rows; join with slip st to **both** loops of first sc, finish off.

Rnd 2: With **wrong** side facing and working in **both** loops, join White with sc in any sc *(see Joining With Sc, page 45)*; sc in each sc around, working 3 sc in center sc of each corner 3-sc group; join with slip st to first sc, finish off.

Rnd 3: With **right** side facing, join Yellow with sc in any sc; sc in each sc around, working 3 sc in center sc of each corner 3-sc group; join with slip st to first sc, finish off.

Rnd 4: With **right** side facing and working in Back Loops Only, join Green with sc in any sc; sc in each sc around, working 3 sc in center sc of each corner 3-sc group; join with slip st to **both** loops of first sc, finish off.

(continued from page 8)

EDGING

Ch 1, turn; sc in first dc, (sc in next ch-1 sp and in next dc) 6 times, 3 sc in next ch-3 sp (top corner), sc in next dc, (sc in next ch-1 sp and in next dc) across; work 13 sc evenly spaced across end of rows, 3 sc in beginning ring (bottom corner), work 13 sc evenly spaced across end of rows; join with slip st to first sc, finish off: 58 sc.

ASSEMBLY

With Blue and working through **both** loops, whipstitch Squares together forming 8 vertical strips of 11 Squares each *(Fig. 7b, page 46)*, beginning in center sc of top corner on one Square and ending in center sc of bottom corner on second Square, then whipstitch strips together in same manner.

BORDER

Rnd 1: With **right** side facing, join Blue with sc in center sc of top corner on last strip *(see Joining With Sc, page 45)*; sc in same sc, work 108 sc evenly spaced across to last sc on last Square, 3 sc in last sc, work 156 sc evenly spaced across to center sc of next corner 3-sc group, 3 sc in center sc, work 108 sc evenly spaced across to last sc on last Square, 3 sc in last sc, work 156 sc evenly spaced across, sc in same sc as first sc; join with slip st to first sc: 540 sc.

Rnd 2: Ch 6 (**counts as first dc plus ch 3**), dc in same sc, ch 3, ★ † (skip next 2 sc, dc in next sc, ch 3) across to within 2 sc of next corner sc, skip next 2 sc †, (dc, ch 3) twice in corner sc; repeat from ★ 2 times **more**, then repeat from † to † once; join with slip st to first dc.

Rnd 3: Slip st in first ch-3 sp, ch 1, (sc, hdc, dc, hdc, sc) in same sp and in each ch-3 sp around; join with slip st to first sc, finish off.

(continued from page 10)

Rnd 4 (Joining rnd): Ch 1, turn; sc in last ch-3 sp made, ★ † ch 3, skip next tr, sc in next sc, (sc, ch 3, sc) in next ch-3 sp, skip next sc, sc in next sc, ch 3 †, (sc, ch 3, sc) in next ch-3 sp; repeat from ★ once **more**, then repeat from † to † once, sc in next ch-3 sp, ch 1, holding Squares with **wrong** sides together, sc in corresponding ch-3 sp on **previous Square**, ch 1, sc in same sp on **new Square**, ch 1, sc in next ch-3 sp on **previous Square**, ch 1, skip next tr on **new Square**, sc in next sc and in next ch-3 sp, ch 1, sc in next ch-3 sp on **previous Square**, ch 1, sc in same sp on **new Square**, skip next sc, sc in next sc, ch 1, sc in next ch-3 sp on **previous Square**, ch 1, sc in same sp as first sc on **new Square**, ch 1, sc in next ch-3 sp on **previous Square**, ch 1; join with slip st to first sc, finish off.

EDGING

With **right** side facing, join yarn with sc in center ch-3 sp at top of First Square *(see Joining With Sc, page 45)*; † ch 3, (sc, ch 5, sc, ch 7, sc, ch 5, sc, ch 3, sc) in same sp, (sc, ch 3, sc) in next 5 ch-3 sps, [sc in next corner ch-3 sp on same Square, ch 3, sc in corner ch-3 sp on next Square, (sc, ch 3, sc) in next 3 ch-3 sps] across to corner ch-3 sp on last Square, (sc, ch 3, sc) in corner ch-3 sp and in next ch-3 sp †, sc in next ch-3 sp, repeat from † to † once; join with slip st to first sc, finish off.

REMAINING 8 STRIPS

Work same as First Strip to Edging.

Instructions continued on page 30.

EDGING

Rnd 1 (Joining rnd): With **right** side facing, join yarn with sc in center ch-3 sp at top of First Square; ch 3, (sc, ch 5, sc, ch 7, sc, ch 5, sc, ch 3, sc) in same sp, (sc, ch 3, sc) in next 5 ch-3 sps, [sc in next corner ch-3 sp on same Square, ch 3, sc in corner ch-3 sp on next Square, (sc, ch 3, sc) in next 3 ch-3 sps] across to corner ch-3 sp on last Square, (sc, ch 3, sc) in corner ch-3 sp and in next ch-3 sp, (sc, ch 3, sc, ch 5, sc, ch 7, sc, ch 5, sc, ch 3, sc) in next ch-3 sp, (sc, ch 3, sc) in next 2 ch-3 sps;

holding Strips with **wrong** sides together, † sc in next ch-3 sp, ch 1, sc in corresponding ch-3 sp on **previous Strip**, ch 1, sc in same sp on **new Strip** †, repeat from † to † 2 times **more**, ★ sc in next corner sp on same Square, ch 1, sc in corresponding ch-3 sp on **previous Strip**, ch 1, sc in corner ch-3 sp on next Square of **new Strip**, repeat from † to † 3 times; repeat from ★ across to next corner ch-3 sp on last Square, (sc, ch 3, sc) in corner ch-3 sp and in next ch-3 sp; join with slip st to first sc, finish off.

June

(continued from page 12)

SQUARE B (Make 20)

Ch 5; join with slip st to form a ring.

Rnd 1 (Right side): Ch 5 (**counts as first hdc plus ch 3**), hdc in ring, ch 1, ★ (hdc, ch 3, hdc) in ring, ch 1; repeat from ★ 2 times **more**; join with slip st to first hdc: 8 hdc and 8 sps.

Note: Mark Rnd 1 as **right** side.

Rnd 2: Slip st in first ch-3 sp, ch 3 (**counts as first hdc plus ch 1, now and throughout**), (hdc, ch 3, hdc, ch 1, hdc) in same sp, ★ ch 1, (hdc, ch 1, hdc, ch 3, hdc, ch 1, hdc) in next ch-3 sp; repeat from ★ 2 times **more**, sc in first hdc to form last ch-1 sp: 16 hdc and 16 sps.

Rnd 3: Ch 3, hdc in last ch-1 sp made, ch 1, (hdc, ch 1, hdc, ch 3, hdc, ch 1, hdc) in next ch-3 sp, ★ ch 1, skip next ch-1 sp, (hdc, ch 1) twice in next ch-1 sp, (hdc, ch 1, hdc, ch 3, hdc, ch 1, hdc) in next ch-3 sp; repeat from ★ 2 times **more**, sc in first hdc to form last ch-1 sp: 24 hdc and 24 sps.

Rnd 4: Ch 3, hdc in last ch-1 sp made, ch 1, skip next ch-1 sp, (hdc, ch 1) twice in next ch-1 sp, (hdc, ch 1, hdc, ch 3, hdc, ch 1, hdc) in next ch-3 sp, ★ ch 1, [skip next ch-1 sp, (hdc, ch 1) twice in next ch-1 sp] twice, (hdc, ch 1, hdc, ch 3, hdc, ch 1, hdc) in next ch-3 sp; repeat from ★ 2 times **more**, sc in first hdc to form last ch-1 sp: 32 hdc and 32 sps.

Rnd 5: Ch 3, hdc in last ch-1 sp made, ch 1, skip next ch-1 sp, 2 hdc in next ch-1 sp, ch 1, skip next ch-1 sp, (hdc, ch 1) twice in next ch-1 sp, ★ † (hdc, ch 1, hdc, ch 2, hdc, ch 1, hdc) in next ch-3 sp, ch 1 †, skip next ch-1 sp, (hdc, ch 1) twice in next ch-1 sp, skip next ch-1 sp, 2 hdc in next ch-1 sp, ch 1, skip next ch-1 sp, (hdc, ch 1) twice in next ch-1 sp; repeat from ★ 2 times **more**, then repeat from † to † once; join with slip st to first hdc, finish off: 40 hdc and 36 sps.

SQUARE C (Make 20)

Ch 5; join with slip st to form a ring.

Rnd 1 (Right side): Ch 5 (**counts as first hdc plus ch 3, now and throughout**), hdc in ring, ch 1, ★ (hdc, ch 3, hdc) in ring, ch 1; repeat from ★ 2 times **more**; join with slip st to first hdc: 8 hdc and 8 sps.

Note: Mark Rnd 1 as **right** side.

Rnd 2: Slip st in first ch-3 sp, ch 5, hdc in same sp, ch 2, slip st in next ch-1 sp, ch 2, ★ (hdc, ch 3, hdc) in next ch-3 sp, ch 2, slip st in next ch-1 sp, ch 2; repeat from ★ 2 times **more**; join with slip st to first hdc: 8 hdc and 12 sps.

Rnd 3: Ch 1, 2 sc in same st, ★ † (2 sc, ch 2, 2 sc) in next ch-3 sp, 2 sc in next hdc, ch 3 †, 2 sc in next hdc; repeat from ★ 2 times **more**, then repeat from † to † once; join with slip st to first sc: 32 sc and 8 sps.

Rnd 4: Ch 4 (**counts as first hdc plus ch 2**), ★ † skip next sc, slip st in next sc, ch 2, (hdc, ch 3, hdc) in next ch-2 sp, ch 2, skip next sc, slip st in next sc, ch 2, skip next sc, hdc in next sc, ch 2, slip st in next ch-3 sp, ch 2 †, hdc in next sc, ch 2; repeat from ★ 2 times **more**, then repeat from † to † once; join with slip st to first hdc: 16 hdc and 28 sps.

Rnd 5: Ch 1, sc in same st, ch 3, ★ † 2 sc in next hdc, (2 sc, ch 2, 2 sc) in next ch-3 sp, 2 sc in next hdc, ch 3 †, (sc in next hdc, ch 3) twice; repeat from ★ 2 times **more**, then repeat from † to † once, sc in next hdc, ch 3; join with slip st to first sc: 40 sc and 16 sps.

Rnd 6: Ch 1, sc in same st, 2 sc in next ch-3 sp, ★ † sc in next 4 sc, (sc, ch 2, sc) in next ch-2 sp, sc in next 4 sc, 2 sc in next ch-3 sp †, (sc in next sc, 2 sc in next ch-3 sp) twice; repeat from ★ 2 times **more**, then repeat from † to † once, sc in next sc, 2 sc in next ch-3 sp; join with slip st to first sc, finish off: 72 sc and 4 ch-2 sps.

ASSEMBLY

Using Placement Diagram as a guide and working through inside loops **only**, whipstitch Squares together forming 9 vertical strips of 9 Squares each *(Fig. 7a, page 46)*, beginning in second ch of first corner ch-2 and ending in first ch of next corner ch-2; then whipstitch strips together in same manner.

Note: There will be a small opening at the corners between Squares.

PLACEMENT DIAGRAM

A	B	A	C	A	B	A	C	A
B	A	C	A	B	A	C	A	B
A	C	A	B	A	C	A	B	A
C	A	B	A	C	A	B	A	C
A	B	A	C	A	B	A	C	A
B	A	C	A	B	A	C	A	B
A	C	A	B	A	C	A	B	A
C	A	B	A	C	A	B	A	C
A	B	A	C	A	B	A	C	A

EDGING

Rnd 1: With **right** side facing, join yarn with sc in any corner ch-2 sp *(see Joining With Sc, page 45)*; ★ † sc in next st and in each st and each joining across to next corner ch-2 sp †, (sc, ch 2, sc) in corner ch-2 sp; repeat from ★ 2 times **more**, then repeat from † to † once, (sc, ch 2) in same sp as first sc; join with slip st to first sc.

Rnd 2: Ch 1, working from **left** to **right**, reverse sc in same st, ch 1, (reverse sc, ch 1) twice in next corner ch-2 sp, ★ (skip next sc, reverse sc in next sc, ch 1) across to next corner ch-2 sp, (reverse sc, ch 1) twice in ch-2 sp; repeat from ★ 2 times **more**, skip next sc, (reverse sc in next sc, ch 1, skip next sc) across; join with slip st to first reverse sc, finish off.

July

(continued from page 14)

Row 10: Ch 1, turn; skip first sc, sc in next 11 sts, 3 sc in next Bobble, sc in next 11 sts, ★ skip next 2 sc, sc in next 11 sts, 3 sc in next Bobble, sc in next 11 sts; repeat from ★ across: 225 sc.

Row 11: Ch 1, turn; skip first sc, ★ † sc in next sc, (ch 1, skip next sc, sc in next sc) 5 times, 3 sc in next sc, sc in next sc, (ch 1, skip next sc, sc in next sc) 5 times †, skip next 2 sc; repeat from ★ 7 times **more**, then repeat from † to † once: 135 sc and 90 ch-1 sps.

Rows 12 and 13: Ch 1, turn; ★ (sc in next ch-1 sp, ch 1) 5 times, skip next sc, sc in next sc, 3 sc in next sc, sc in next sc, (ch 1, sc in next ch-1 sp) 5 times; repeat from ★ across.

Row 14: Ch 1, turn; ★ (sc in next ch-1 sp, ch 1) 5 times, skip next sc, sc in next sc, 3 sc in next sc, sc in next sc, (ch 1, sc in next ch-1 sp) 5 times; repeat from ★ across, changing to Blue in last sc.

Row 15: Ch 1, turn; ★ (sc in next ch-1 sp, ch 1) 5 times, skip next sc, sc in next sc, 3 sc in next sc, sc in next sc, (ch 1, sc in next ch-1 sp) 5 times; repeat from ★ across, changing to Red in last sc.

Row 16: Ch 1, turn; ★ (sc in next ch-1 sp, ch 1) 5 times, skip next sc, sc in next sc, 3 sc in next sc, sc in next sc, (ch 1, sc in next ch-1 sp) 5 times; repeat from ★ across, changing to Blue in last sc.

Row 17: Ch 1, turn; ★ (sc in next ch-1 sp, ch 1) 5 times, skip next sc, sc in next sc, 3 sc in next sc, sc in next sc, (ch 1, sc in next ch-1 sp) 5 times; repeat from ★ across, changing to White in last sc.

Rows 18-31: Ch 1, turn; ★ (sc in next ch-1 sp, ch 1) 5 times, skip next sc, sc in next sc, 3 sc in next sc, sc in next sc, (ch 1, sc in next ch-1 sp) 5 times; repeat from ★ across.

Rows 32-35: Repeat Rows 14-17.

Rows 36-39: Ch 1, turn; ★ (sc in next ch-1 sp, ch 1) 5 times, skip next sc, sc in next sc, 3 sc in next sc, sc in next sc, (ch 1, sc in next ch-1 sp) 5 times; repeat from ★ across.

Row 40: Ch 1, turn; ★ (sc in next ch-1 sp, ch 1) 5 times, skip next sc, sc in next sc, 3 sc in next sc, sc in next sc, (ch 1, sc in next ch-1 sp) 5 times; repeat from ★ across, changing to Blue in last sc.

Rows 41-139: Repeat Rows 9-40, 3 times; then repeat Rows 9-11 once **more**.

Rows 140-145: Ch 1, turn; ★ (sc in next ch-1 sp, ch 1) 5 times, skip next sc, sc in next sc, 3 sc in next sc, sc in next sc, (ch 1, sc in next ch-1 sp) 5 times; repeat from ★ across.

Do **not** finish off.

EDGING

Ch 1, do **not** turn; sc evenly spaced across end of rows; working in free loops and sps of beginning ch *(Fig. 4b, page 45)*, 3 sc in first ch, sc in next 10 chs, skip next ch, ★ sc in next 11 chs, 3 sc in next sp, sc in next 11 chs, skip next ch; repeat from ★ 7 times **more**, sc in next 10 chs, 3 sc in last ch; sc evenly spaced across end of rows; join with slip st to first sc on Row 145, finish off.

Rnd 8: Ch 2, ★ † work FPdc around each of next 3 sts, sc in Back Loop Only of next 9 sc, work FPdc around each of next 3 sts †, (hdc, ch 1, hdc) in next ch-1 sp; repeat from ★ 2 times **more**, then repeat from † to † once, hdc in same sp as first hdc, sc in first hdc to form last ch-1 sp: 68 sts and 4 ch-1 sps.

Rnd 9: Ch 2, ★ † work FPdc around each of next 4 sts, sc in Back Loop Only of next 9 sc, work FPdc around each of next 4 sts †, (hdc, ch 1, hdc) in next ch-1 sp; repeat from ★ 2 times **more**, then repeat from † to † once, hdc in same sp as first hdc, sc in first hdc to form last ch-1 sp: 76 sts and 4 ch-1 sps.

Rnd 10: Ch 2, ★ † work FPdc around each of next 5 sts, sc in Back Loop Only of next 9 sc, work FPdc around each of next 5 sts †, (hdc, ch 1, hdc) in next ch-1 sp; repeat from ★ 2 times **more**, then repeat from † to † once, hdc in same sp as first hdc, sc in first hdc to form last ch-1 sp: 84 sts and 4 ch-1 sps.

Rnd 11: Ch 2, ★ † work FPdc around each of next 6 sts, sc in Back Loop Only of next 9 sc, work FPdc around each of next 6 sts †, (hdc, ch 1, hdc) in next ch-1 sp; repeat from ★ 2 times **more**, then repeat from † to † once, hdc in same sp as first hdc, sc in first hdc to form last ch-1 sp: 92 sts and 4 ch-1 sps.

Rnd 12: Ch 2, ★ † work FPdc around each of next 7 sts, sc in Back Loop Only of next 9 sc, work FPdc around each of next 7 sts †, (hdc, ch 1, hdc) in next ch-1 sp; repeat from ★ 2 times **more**, then repeat from † to † once, hdc in same sp as first hdc, sc in first hdc to form last ch-1 sp: 100 sts and 4 ch-1 sps.

Rnd 13: Ch 2, ★ † work FPdc around each of next 8 sts, sc in Back Loop Only of next 9 sc, work FPdc around each of next 8 sts †, (hdc, ch 1, hdc) in next ch-1 sp; repeat from ★ 2 times **more**, then repeat from † to † once, hdc in same sp as first hdc, sc in first hdc to form last ch-1 sp: 108 sts and 4 ch-1 sps.

Rnd 14: Ch 2, ★ † sc in Back Loop Only of next 9 sts, hdc in **both** loops of next 9 sc, sc in Back Loop Only of next 9 sts †, (hdc, ch 1, hdc) in next ch-1 sp; repeat from ★ 2 times **more**, then repeat from † to † once, hdc in same sp as first hdc, sc in first hdc to form last ch-1 sp: 116 sts and 4 ch-1 sps.

Rnd 15: Ch 2, ★ † work FPdc around next st, sc in Back Loop Only of next 9 sc, work FPdc around each of next 9 sts, sc in Back Loop Only of next 9 sc, work FPdc around next st †, (hdc, ch 1, hdc) in next ch-1 sp; repeat from ★ 2 times **more**, then repeat from † to † once, hdc in same sp as first hdc, sc in first hdc to form last ch-1 sp: 124 sts and 4 ch-1 sps.

Rnd 16: Ch 2, ★ † work FPdc around each of next 2 sts, sc in Back Loop Only of next 9 sc, work FPdc around each of next 9 FPdc, sc in Back Loop Only of next 9 sc, work FPdc around each of next 2 sts †, (hdc, ch 1, hdc) in next ch-1 sp; repeat from ★ 2 times **more**, then repeat from † to † once, hdc in same sp as first hdc, sc in first hdc to form last ch-1 sp: 132 sts and 4 ch-1 sps.

Rnd 17: Ch 2, ★ † work FPdc around each of next 3 sts, sc in Back Loop Only of next 9 sc, work FPdc around each of next 9 FPdc, sc in Back Loop Only of next 9 sc, work FPdc around each of next 3 sts †, (hdc, ch 1, hdc) in next ch-1 sp; repeat from ★ 2 times **more**, then repeat from † to † once, hdc in same sp as first hdc, sc in first hdc to form last ch-1 sp: 140 sts and 4 ch-1 sps.

Rnd 18: Ch 2, ★ † work FPdc around each of next 4 sts, sc in Back Loop Only of next 9 sc, work FPdc around each of next 9 FPdc, sc in Back Loop Only of next 9 sc, work FPdc around each of next 4 sts †, (hdc, ch 1, hdc) in next ch-1 sp; repeat from ★ 2 times **more**, then repeat from † to † once, hdc in same sp as first hdc, sc in first hdc to form last ch-1 sp: 148 sts and 4 ch-1 sps.

Instructions continued on page 34.

Rnd 19: Ch 2, ★ † work FPdc around each of next 5 sts, sc in Back Loop Only of next 9 sc, work FPdc around each of next 9 FPdc, sc in Back Loop Only of next 9 sc, work FPdc around each of next 5 sts †, (hdc, ch 1, hdc) in next ch-1 sp; repeat from ★ 2 times **more**, then repeat from † to † once, hdc in same sp as first hdc, sc in first hdc to form last ch-1 sp: 156 sts and 4 ch-1 sps.

Rnd 20: Ch 2, ★ † work FPdc around each of next 6 sts, sc in Back Loop Only of next 9 sc, work FPdc around each of next 9 FPdc, sc in Back Loop Only of next 9 sc, work FPdc around each of next 6 sts †, (hdc, ch 1, hdc) in next ch-1 sp; repeat from ★ 2 times **more**, then repeat from † to † once, hdc in same sp as first hdc, sc in first hdc to form last ch-1 sp: 164 sts and 4 ch-1 sps.

Rnd 21: Ch 2, ★ † work FPdc around each of next 7 sts, sc in Back Loop Only of next 9 sc, work FPdc around each of next 9 FPdc, sc in Back Loop Only of next 9 sc, work FPdc around each of next 7 sts †, (hdc, ch 1, hdc) in next ch-1 sp; repeat from ★ 2 times **more**, then repeat from † to † once, hdc in same sp as first hdc, sc in first hdc to form last ch-1 sp: 172 sts and 4 ch-1 sps.

Rnd 22: Ch 2, ★ † work FPdc around each of next 8 sts, sc in Back Loop Only of next 9 sc, work FPdc around each of next 9 FPdc, sc in Back Loop Only of next 9 sc, work FPdc around each of next 8 sts †, (hdc, ch 1, hdc) in next ch-1 sp; repeat from ★ 2 times **more**, then repeat from † to † once, hdc in same sp as first hdc, sc in first hdc to form last ch-1 sp: 180 sts and 4 ch-1 sps.

Rnd 23: Ch 2, ★ † sc in Back Loop Only of next 9 sts, (hdc in **both** loops of next 9 sc, sc in Back Loop Only of next 9 sts) twice †, (hdc, ch 1, hdc) in next ch-1 sp; repeat from ★ 2 times **more**, then repeat from † to † once, hdc in same sp as first hdc, sc in first hdc to form last ch-1 sp: 188 sts and 4 ch-1 sps.

Rnd 24: Ch 2, ★ † work FPdc around next st, sc in Back Loop Only of next 9 sc, (work FPdc around each of next 9 hdc, sc in Back Loop Only of next 9 sc) twice, work FPdc around next hdc †, (hdc, ch 1, hdc) in next ch-1 sp; repeat from ★ 2 times

more, then repeat from † to † once, hdc in same sp as first hdc, sc in first hdc to form last ch-1 sp: 196 sts and 4 ch-1 sps.

Rnd 25: Ch 2, ★ † work FPdc around each of next 2 sts, sc in Back Loop Only of next 9 sc, (work FPdc around each of next 9 FPdc, sc in Back Loop Only of next 9 sc) twice, work FPdc around each of next 2 sts †, (hdc, ch 1, hdc) in next ch-1 sp; repeat from ★ 2 times **more**, then repeat from † to † once, hdc in same sp as first hdc, sc in first hdc to form last ch-1 sp: 204 sts and 4 ch-1 sps.

Rnd 26: Ch 2, ★ † work FPdc around each of next 3 sts, sc in Back Loop Only of next 9 sc, (work FPdc around each of next 9 FPdc, sc in Back Loop Only of next 9 sc) twice, work FPdc around each of next 3 sts †, (hdc, ch 1, hdc) in next ch-1 sp; repeat from ★ 2 times **more**, then repeat from † to † once, hdc in same sp as first hdc, sc in first hdc to form last ch-1 sp: 212 sts and 4 ch-1 sps.

Rnd 27: Ch 2, ★ † work FPdc around each of next 4 sts, sc in Back Loop Only of next 9 sc, (work FPdc around each of next 9 FPdc, sc in Back Loop Only of next 9 sc) twice, work FPdc around each of next 4 sts †, (hdc, ch 1, hdc) in next ch-1 sp; repeat from ★ 2 times **more**, then repeat from † to † once, hdc in same sp as first hdc, sc in first hdc to form last ch-1 sp: 220 sts and 4 ch-1 sps.

When working a dc in the free loop of a st *(Fig. 4a, page 45)*, work in **front** of previous rnd *(Fig. 2, page 45)*. Skip next st on previous rnd (**behind** dc).

Rnd 28: Ch 2, † work FPdc around each of next 5 sts, sc in Back Loop Only of next 9 sc, (work FPdc around each of next 9 FPdc, sc in Back Loop Only of next 9 sc) twice, work FPdc around each of next 5 sts, (hdc, ch 1, hdc) in next ch-1 sp, work FPdc around each of next 5 sts, sc in Back Loop Only of next 3 sc, dc in free loop of next sc on Rnd 26, sc in Back Loop Only of next 5 sc, (work FPdc around each of next 9 FPdc, sc in Back Loop Only of next 9 sc) twice, work FPdc around each of next 5 sts †, (hdc, ch 1, hdc) in next ch-1 sp; repeat from † to † once, hdc in same sp as first hdc, sc in first hdc to form last ch-1 sp: 228 sts and 4 ch-1 sps.

Rnd 29: Ch 2, † work FPdc around each of next 6 sts, sc in Back Loop Only of next 9 sc, (work FPdc around each of next 9 FPdc, sc in Back Loop Only of next 9 sc) twice, work FPdc around each of next 6 sts, (hdc, ch 1, hdc) in next ch-1 sp, work FPdc around each of next 6 sts, sc in Back Loop Only of next sc, dc in free loop of next 2 sc on Rnd 27, work FPdc around next dc, dc in free loop of next sc on Rnd 27, sc in Back Loop Only of next 4 sc, (work FPdc around each of next 9 FPdc, sc in Back Loop Only of next 9 sc) twice, work FPdc around each of next 6 sts †, (hdc, ch 1, hdc) in next ch-1 sp; repeat from † to † once, hdc in same sp as first hdc, sc in first hdc to form last ch-1 sp: 236 sts and 4 ch-1 sps.

Rnd 30: Ch 2, † work FPdc around each of next 7 sts, sc in Back Loop Only of next 9 sc, (work FPdc around each of next 9 FPdc, sc in Back Loop Only of next 9 sc) twice, work FPdc around each of next 7 sts, (hdc, ch 1, hdc) in next ch-1 sp, work FPdc around each of next 7 sts, sc in Back Loop Only of next 2 sts, work FPdc around each of next 2 sts, sc in Back Loop Only of next dc, dc in free loop of next sc on Rnd 28, sc in Back Loop Only of next 3 sc, (work FPdc around each of next 9 FPdc, sc in Back Loop Only of next 9 sc) twice, work FPdc around each of next 7 sts †, (hdc, ch 1, hdc) in next ch-1 sp; repeat from † to † once, hdc in same sp as first hdc, sc in first hdc to form last ch-1 sp: 244 sts and 4 ch-1 sps.

Rnd 31: Ch 2, † work FPdc around each of next 8 sts, sc in Back Loop Only of next 9 sc, (work FPdc around each of next 9 FPdc, sc in Back Loop Only of next 9 sc) twice, work FPdc around each of next 8 sts, (hdc, ch 1, hdc) in next ch-1 sp, work FPdc around each of next 8 sts, sc in Back Loop Only of next sc, dc in free loop of next dc on Rnd 29, work FPdc around each of next 2 FPdc, dc in free loop of next dc on Rnd 29, work FPdc around next dc, dc in free loop of next 2 sc on Rnd 29, sc in Back Loop Only of next sc, (work FPdc around each of next 9 FPdc, sc in Back Loop Only of next 9 sc) twice, work FPdc around each of next 8 sts †, (hdc, ch 1, hdc) in next ch-1 sp; repeat from † to † once, hdc in same sp as first hdc, sc in first hdc to form last ch-1 sp: 252 sts and 4 ch-1 sps.

Rnd 32: Ch 3 (**counts as first hdc plus ch 1**), † hdc in Back Loop Only of next hdc, ch 1, (skip next st, hdc in Back Loop Only of next st, ch 1) across to next ch-1 sp, (hdc, ch 1) twice in next ch-1 sp, hdc in Back Loop Only of next hdc, (ch 1, skip next FPdc, hdc in Back Loop Only of next FPdc) 4 times, dc in free loop of next sc on Rnd 30, work FPdc around each of next 3 sts, sc in Back Loop Only of next 2 sts, work FPdc around each of next 2 dc, ch 1, (skip next st, hdc in Back Loop of next st, ch 1) across to next ch-1 sp †, (hdc, ch 1) twice in next ch-1 sp; repeat from † to † once, hdc in same sp as first hdc, sc in first hdc to form last ch-1 sp: 144 sts and 128 ch-1 sps.

Rnd 33: Ch 2, † sc in Back Loop Only of each st and each ch across to next corner ch-1 sp, (hdc, ch 1, hdc) in corner ch-1 sp, (sc in Back Loop Only of next hdc and in next ch) 5 times, work FPdc around each of next 4 sts, sc in Back Loop Only of each st and ch across to next corner ch-1 sp †, (hdc, ch 1, hdc) in corner ch-1 sp; repeat from † to † once, hdc in same sp as first hdc, sc in first hdc to form last ch-1 sp: 276 sts and 4 ch-1 sps.

Rnd 34: Ch 2, † sc in Back Loop Only of each st across to next ch-1 sp, (hdc, ch 1, hdc) in next ch-1 sp, sc in Back Loop Only of next 11 sts, work FPdc around each of next 4 FPdc, sc in Back Loop Only of each st across to next ch-1 sp †, (hdc, ch 1, hdc) in next ch-1 sp; repeat from † to † once, hdc in same sp as first hdc, sc in first hdc to form last ch-1 sp: 284 sts and 4 ch-1 sps.

Rnd 35: Ch 2, † sc in Back Loop Only of each st across to next ch-1 sp, (hdc, ch 1, hdc) in next ch-1 sp, sc in Back Loop Only of next 11 sts, dc in free loop of next sc on Rnd 33, work FPdc around each of next 3 FPdc, sc in Back Loop Only of each st across to next ch-1 sp †, (hdc, ch 1, hdc) in next ch-1 sp; repeat from † to † once, hdc in same sp as first hdc, sc in first hdc to form last ch-1 sp: 292 sts and 4 ch-1 sps.

Rnd 36: Ch 2, † sc in Back Loop Only of each st across to next ch-1 sp, (hdc, ch 1, hdc) in next ch-1 sp, sc in Back Loop Only of next 12 sts, work FPdc around each of next 4 sts, sc in Back Loop Only of each st across to next ch-1 sp †, (hdc, ch 1, hdc) in next ch-1 sp; repeat from † to † once, hdc in same sp as first hdc, sc in first hdc to form last ch-1 sp: 300 sts and 4 ch-1 sps.

Instructions continued on page 36.

Rnd 37: Ch 2, † sc in Back Loop Only of each st across to next ch-1 sp, (hdc, ch 1, hdc) in next ch-1 sp, sc in Back Loop Only of next 12 sts, dc in free loop of next sc on Rnd 35, work FPdc around each of next 3 FPdc, sc in Back Loop Only of each st across to next ch-1 sp †, (hdc, ch 1, hdc) in next ch-1 sp; repeat from † to † once, hdc in same sp as first hdc, sc in first hdc to form last ch-1 sp: 308 sts and 4 ch-1 sps.

Rnd 38: Ch 2, † sc in Back Loop Only of next 4 sts, dc in free loop of next 10 sc on Rnd 36, sc in Back Loop Only of next sc, dc in free loop of next 7 sc on Rnd 36, sc in Back Loop only of each st across to next ch-1 sp, (hdc, ch 1, hdc) in next ch-1 sp, sc in Back Loop Only of next 13 sts, work FPdc around each of next 4 sts, sc in Back Loop Only of each st across to next ch-1 sp †, (hdc, ch 1, hdc) in next ch-1 sp; repeat from † to † once, hdc in same sp as first hdc, sc in first hdc to form last ch-1 sp: 316 sts and 4 ch-1 sps.

Rnd 39: Ch 2, † sc in Back Loop Only of next 5 sts, work FPdc around each of next 9 dc, sc in Back Loop Only of next dc, dc in free loop of next sc on Rnd 37, work FPdc around each of next 7 dc, dc in free loop of next sc on Rnd 37, sc in Back Loop Only of next 8 sc, dc in free loop of next 3 sc on Rnd 37, sc in Back Loop Only of each st across to next ch-1 sp, (hdc, ch 1, hdc) in next ch-1 sp, sc in Back Loop Only of next 13 sts, dc in free loop of next sc on Rnd 37, work FPdc around each of next 4 FPdc, sc in Back Loop Only of each st across to next ch-1 sp †, (hdc, ch 1, hdc) in next ch-1 sp; repeat from † to † once, hdc in same sp as first hdc, sc in first hdc to form last ch-1 sp: 324 sts and 4 ch-1 sps.

Rnd 40: Ch 2, † sc in Back Loop Only of next 4 sts, dc in free loop of next 2 sc on Rnd 38, (work FPdc around each of next 9 sts, dc in free loop of next st on Rnd 38) twice, sc in Back Loop Only of next 6 sts, dc in free loop of next sc on Rnd 38, sc in Back Loop Only of each st across to next ch-1 sp, (hdc, ch 1, hdc) in next ch-1 sp, sc in Back Loop Only of next 13 sts, dc in free loop of next sc on Rnd 38, work FPdc around each of next 5 sts, sc in Back Loop Only of each st across to next ch-1 sp †, (hdc, ch 1, hdc) in next ch-1 sp; repeat from † to † once, hdc in same sp as first hdc, sc in first hdc to form last ch-1 sp: 332 sts and 4 ch-1 sps.

Rnd 41: Ch 2, † sc in Back Loop Only of next 4 sts, dc in free loop of next sc on Rnd 39, sc in Back Loop Only of next dc, work FPdc around each of next 9 sts, sc in Back Loop Only of next FPdc, work FPdc around each of next 11 sts, sc in Back Loop Only of next 5 sc, dc in free loop of next sc on Rnd 39, sc in Back Loop Only of each st across to next ch-1 sp, (hdc, ch 1, hdc) in next ch-1 sp, sc in Back Loop Only of next 12 sts, dc in free loop of next 2 sc on Rnd 39, work FPdc around each of next 5 sts, sc in Back Loop Only of next 24 sts, dc in free loop of next 6 sc on Rnd 39, sc in Back Loop Only of next 14 sc, dc in free loop of next 3 sc on Rnd 39, sc in Back Loop Only of each st across to next ch-1 sp †, (hdc, ch 1, hdc) in next ch-1 sp; repeat from † to † once, hdc in same sp as first hdc, sc in first hdc to form last ch-1 sp: 340 sts and 4 ch-1 sps.

Rnd 42: Ch 2, † sc in Back Loop Only of next 5 sts, work FPdc around next dc, sc in Back Loop Only of next sc, work FPdc around each of next 9 FPdc, sc in Back Loop Only of next sc, work FPdc around each of next 11 FPdc, dc in free loop of next sc on Rnd 40, sc in Back Loop Only of next 3 sc, dc in free loop of next sc on Rnd 40, sc in Back Loop Only of each st across to next ch-1 sp, (hdc, ch 1, hdc) in next ch-1 sp, sc in Back Loop Only of next 9 sts, dc in free loop of next 4 sc on Rnd 40, work FPdc around each of next 7 sts, sc in Back Loop Only of next 18 sc, dc in free loop of next 6 sc on Rnd 40, work FPdc around each of next 6 dc, dc in free loop of next 2 sc on Rnd 40, sc in Back Loop Only of next 10 sc, dc in free loop of next 2 sc on Rnd 40, sc in Back Loop Only of next dc, work FPdc around each of next 2 dc, sc in Back Loop Only of each st across to next ch-1 sp †, (hdc, ch 1, hdc) in next ch-1 sp; repeat from † to † once, hdc in same sp as first hdc, sc in first hdc to form last ch-1 sp: 348 sts and 4 ch-1 sps.

Rnd 43: Ch 2, † sc in Back Loop Only of next 6 sts, work FPdc around next FPdc, sc in Back Loop Only of next sc, (work FPdc around each of next 9 FPdc, sc in Back Loop Only of next st) twice, work FPdc around each of next 2 sts, sc in Back Loop Only of next 3 sc, work FPdc around next dc, sc in Back Loop Only of next 36 sts, dc in free loop of next 6 sc on Rnd 41, sc in each st across to next ch-1 sp, (hdc, ch 1, hdc) in next ch-1 sp, sc in Back Loop Only of next 8 sts, dc in free loop of next 2 sc on Rnd 41, work FPdc around each of next 11 sts, sc in Back Loop Only of next 16 sc, dc in free loop of next 2 sc on Rnd 41, work FPdc around each of next 14 sts, dc in free loop of next sc on Rnd 41, sc in Back Loop Only of next 8 sc, dc in free loop of next sc on Rnd 41, sc in Back Loop Only of next 12 sts, dc in free loop of next 6 sc on Rnd 41, sc in Back Loop Only of each st across to next ch-1 sp †, (hdc, ch 1, hdc) in next ch-1 sp; repeat from † to † once, hdc in same sp as first hdc, sc in first sc to form last ch-1 sp: 356 sts and 4 ch-1 sps.

Rnd 44: Ch 2, † sc in Back Loop Only of next 7 sts, work FPdc around next FPdc, sc in Back Loop Only of next sc, work FPdc around each of next 9 FPdc, dc in free loop of next sc on Rnd 42, sc in Back Loop Only of next FPdc, work FPdc around each of next 8 FPdc, dc in free loop of next FPdc on Rnd 42, work FPdc around each of next 2 FPdc, sc in Back Loop Only of next 3 sc, work FPdc around next FPdc, sc in Back Loop Only of next 29 sts, dc in free loop of next 7 sc on Rnd 42, work FPdc around each of next 6 FPdc, dc in free loop of next sc on Rnd 42, sc in Back Loop only of next sc, dc in free loop of next sc on Rnd 42, sc in Back Loop Only of next 4 sc, dc in free loop of next sc on Rnd 42, sc in Back Loop Only of each st across to next ch-1 sp, (hdc, ch 1, hdc) in next ch-1 sp, sc in Back Loop Only of next 8 sts, dc in free loop of next sc on Rnd 42, sc in Back Loop Only of next dc, work FPdc around each of next 12 FPdc, sc in Back Loop Only of next 14 sc, dc in free loop of next 2 sc on Rnd 42, work FPdc around each of next 13 sts, sc in Back Loop Only of next FPdc, work FPdc around each of next 3 sts, sc in Back Loop Only of next 8 sc, work FPdc around next dc, sc in Back Loop Only of next 10 sc, dc in free loop of next 2 sc on Rnd 42, work FPdc around each of next 3 dc, sc in Back Loop Only of next dc, work FPdc around each of next 2 dc, dc in free loop of next sc on Rnd 42, sc in Back Loop Only of each st across to next ch-1 sp †, (hdc, ch 1, hdc) in next ch-1 sp; repeat from † to † once, hdc in same sp as first hdc, sc in first hdc to form last ch-1 sp: 364 sts and 4 ch-1 sps.

Rnd 45: Ch 2, † sc in Back Loop Only of next 8 sts, work FPdc around next FPdc, sc in Back Loop Only of next sc, work FPdc around each of next 10 sts, sc in Back Loop Only of next sc, work FPdc around each of next 11 sts, sc in Back Loop Only of next 4 sts, dc in free loop of next sc on Rnd 43, sc in Back Loop Only of next 19 sc, dc in free loop of next sc on Rnd 43, sc in Back Loop Only of next 7 sc, dc in free loop of next sc on Rnd 43, work FPdc around each of next 14 sts, dc in free loop of next sc on Rnd 43, sc in Back Loop Only of next dc, dc in free loop of next sc on Rnd 43, sc in Back Loop Only of next 2 sc, dc in free loop of next sc on Rnd 43, sc in Back Loop Only of each st across to next ch-1 sp, (hdc, ch 1, hdc) in next ch-1 sp, sc in Back Loop Only of next 9 sts, work FPdc around next dc, sc in Back Loop Only of next sc, work FPdc around each of next 11 FPdc, sc in Back Loop Only of next 14 sts, dc in free loop of next sc on Rnd 43, work FPdc around each of next 15 sts, sc in Back Loop Only of next sc, work FPdc around each of next 3 FPdc, dc in free loop of next st on Rnd 43, sc in Back Loop Only of next 8 sts, dc in free loop of next dc on Rnd 43, sc in Back Loop Only of next sc, dc in free loop of next 8 sc on Rnd 43, sc in Back Loop Only of next dc, work FPdc around each of next 4 sts, sc in Back Loop Only of next sc, work FPdc around each of next 3 sts, dc in free loop of next sc on Rnd 43, sc in Back Loop Only of each st across to next ch-1 sp †, (hdc, ch 1, hdc) in next ch-1 sp; repeat from † to † once, hdc in same sp as first hdc, sc in first hdc to form last ch-1 sp: 372 sts and 4 ch-1 sps.

Instructions continued on page 38.

Rnd 46: Ch 2, † sc in Back Loop Only of next 9 sts, work FPdc around next FPdc, sc in Back Loop Only of next sc, work FPdc around each of next 10 FPdc, dc in free loop of next sc on Rnd 44, sc in Back Loop Only of next FPdc, work FPdc around each of next 10 FPdc, sc in Back Loop Only of next 5 sts, dc in free loop of next sc on Rnd 44, sc in Back Loop Only of next 15 sc, dc in free loop of next 3 sc on Rnd 44, work FPdc around next dc, dc in free loop of next sc on Rnd 44, sc in Back Loop Only of next 5 sc, dc in free loop of next sc on Rnd 44, work FPdc around each of next 16 sts, dc in free loop of next dc on Rnd 44, work FPdc around next dc, dc in free loop of next 2 sc on Rnd 44, work FPdc around next dc, sc in Back Loop Only of each st across to next ch-1 sp, (hdc, ch 1, hdc) in next ch-1 sp, sc in Back Loop Only of next 9 sts, dc in free loop of next sc on Rnd 44, work FPdc around next FPdc, sc in Back Loop Only of next sc, work FPdc around each of next 11 FPdc, sc in Back Loop Only of next 13 sc, dc in free loop of next sc on Rnd 44, work FPdc around each of next 16 sts, dc in free loop of next sc on Rnd 44, work FPdc around each of next 4 sts, sc in Back Loop Only of next 9 sts, dc in free loop of next sc on Rnd 44, work FPdc around each of next 8 dc, sc in Back Loop Only of next sc, work FPdc around each of next 4 FPdc, dc in free loop of next sc on Rnd 44, work FPdc around each of next 3 FPdc, sc in Back Loop Only of next dc, dc in free loop of next sc on Rnd 44, sc in Back Loop Only of each st across to next ch-1 sp †, (hdc, ch 1, hdc) in next ch-1 sp; repeat from † to † once, hdc in same sp as first hdc, sc in first hdc to form last ch-1 sp: 380 sts and 4 ch-1 sps.

Rnd 47: Ch 2, † sc in Back Loop Only of next 9 sts, dc in free loop of next sc on Rnd 45, sc in Back Loop Only of next 2 sts, work FPdc around each of next 11 sts, dc in free loop of next FPdc on Rnd 45, sc in Back Loop Only of next 2 FPdc, work FPdc around each of next 4 FPdc, sc in Back Loop Only of next FPdc, work FPdc around each of next 3 FPdc, sc in Back Loop Only of next 6 sts, dc in free loop of next 15 sc on Rnd 45, work FPdc around each of next 4 sts, sc in Back Loop Only of next dc, dc in free loop of next sc on Rnd 45, sc in Back Loop Only of next 4 sc, work FPdc around each of next 22 sts, sc in Back Loop Only of next sc, dc in free loop of next sc on Rnd 45, sc in Back

Loop Only of each st across to next ch-1 sp, (hdc, ch 1, hdc) in next ch-1 sp, sc in Back Loop Only of next 13 sts, work FPdc around each of next 3 FPdc, sc in Back Loop Only of next 4 FPdc, work FPdc around each of next 4 FPdc, sc in Back Loop Only of next 12 sc, dc in free loop of next sc on Rnd 45, work FPdc around each of next 20 sts, sc in Back Loop Only of next FPdc, work FPdc around next FPdc, sc in Back Loop Only of next 10 sts, work FPdc around each of next 8 FPdc, dc in free loop of next sc on Rnd 45, sc in Back Loop Only of next FPdc, work FPdc around each of next 7 sts, dc in free loop of next dc on Rnd 45, work FPdc around next dc, dc in free loop of next sc on Rnd 45, sc in Back Loop Only of each st across to next ch-1 sp †, (hdc, ch 1, hdc) in next ch-1 sp; repeat from † to † once, hdc in same sp as first hdc, sc in first hdc to form last ch-1 sp: 388 sts and 4 ch-1 sps.

Rnd 48: Ch 2, † sc in Back Loop Only of next 10 sts, work FPdc around next dc, sc in Back Loop Only of next 2 sc, work FPdc around each of next 12 sts, dc in free loop of next 2 FPdc on Rnd 46, work FPdc around each of next 4 FPdc, sc in Back Loop Only of next sc, work FPdc around each of next 3 FPdc, sc in Back Loop Only of next 7 sts, work FPdc around each of next 18 sts, dc in free loop of next dc on Rnd 46, work FPdc around next dc, dc in free loop of next sc on Rnd 46, sc in Back Loop Only of next 3 sc, work FPdc around each of next 20 FPdc, sc in Back Loop Only of next FPdc, work FPdc around next FPdc, dc in free loop of next sc on Rnd 46, work FPdc around next dc, sc in Back Loop Only of each st across to next ch-1 sp, (hdc, ch 1, hdc) in next ch-1 sp, sc in Back Loop Only of next 14 sts, work FPdc around each of next 3 FPdc, sc in Back Loop Only of next 4 sc, work FPdc around each of next 4 FPdc, sc in Back Loop Only of next 12 sc, work FPdc around each of next 21 sts, dc in free loop of next FPdc on Rnd 46, work FPdc around next FPdc, sc in Back Loop Only of next 9 sc, dc in free loop of next dc on Rnd 46, work FPdc around each of next 9 sts, sc in Back Loop Only of next sc, work FPdc around each of next 10 sts, sc in Back Loop Only of each st across to next ch-1 sp †, (hdc, ch 1, hdc) in next ch-1 sp; repeat from † to † once, hdc in same sp as first hdc, sc in first hdc to form last ch-1 sp: 396 sts and 4 ch-1 sps.

Rnd 49: Ch 2, † sc in Back Loop Only of next 14 sts, work FPdc around each of next 18 sts, sc in Back Loop Only of next 2 sts, work FPdc around each of next 2 FPdc, sc in Back Loop Only of next 6 sc, dc in free loop of next sc on Rnd 47, work FPdc around each of next 21 sts, sc in Back Loop Only of next 3 sc, work FPdc around each of next 20 FPdc, dc in free loop of next dc on Rnd 47, work FPdc around each of next 3 sts, dc in free loop of next sc on Rnd 47, sc in Back Loop Only of each st across to next ch-1 sp, (hdc, ch 1, hdc) in next ch-1 sp, sc in Back Loop Only of next 15 sts, work FPdc around each of next 2 FPdc, sc in Back Loop Only of next 5 sts, work FPdc around each of next 2 FPdc, sc in Back Loop Only of next FPdc, work FPdc around next FPdc, sc in Back Loop Only of next 12 sc, work FPdc around each of next 17 FPdc, sc in Back Loop Only of next FPdc, work FPdc around each of next 5 sts, sc in Back Loop Only of next 9 sc, work FPdc around each of next 10 sts, dc in free loop of next sc on Rnd 47, sc in Back Loop Only of next FPdc, work FPdc around each of next 4 FPdc, sc in Back Loop Only of next 3 FPdc, work FPdc around next st, sc in Back Loop Only of each st across to next ch-1 sp †, (hdc, ch 1, hdc) in next ch-1 sp; repeat from † to † once, hdc in same sp as first hdc, sc in first hdc to form last ch-1 sp: 404 sts and 4 ch-1 sps.

Rnd 50: Ch 2, † sc in Back Loop Only of next 15 sts, work FPdc around each of next 8 FPdc, sc in Back Loop Only of next 3 FPdc, work FPdc around each of next 7 FPdc, sc in Back Loop Only of next 2 sc, work FPdc around each of next 2 FPdc, sc in Back Loop Only of next 6 sc, work FPdc around each of next 18 sts, sc in Back Loop Only of next 2 FPdc, work FPdc around next FPdc, sc in Back Loop Only of next 4 sts, work FPdc around each of next 25 sts, sc in Back Loop Only of each st across to next ch-1 sp, (hdc, ch 1, hdc) in next ch-1 sp, sc in Back Loop Only of next 15 sts, dc in free loop of next sc on Rnd 48, sc in Back Loop Only of next FPdc, work FPdc around next FPdc, sc in Back Loop Only of next 6 sts, work FPdc around next FPdc, sc in Back Loop Only of next sc, work FPdc around next FPdc, dc in free loop of next sc on Rnd 48, sc in Back Loop Only of next 11 sc, work FPdc around each of next 15 FPdc, sc in Back Loop Only of next 6 sts, work FPdc around each of next 2 FPdc, sc in Back Loop Only of next 9 sc, work FPdc around each of next 11 sts, dc in free loop of next FPdc on Rnd 48, sc in Back Loop Only of next FPdc, work FPdc around each of next 2 FPdc, sc in Back Loop Only of each st across to next ch-1 sp †, (hdc, ch 1, hdc) in next ch-1 sp; repeat from † to † once, hdc in same sp as first hdc, sc in first hdc to form last ch-1 sp: 412 sts and 4 ch-1 sps.

Rnd 51: Ch 2, † sc in Back Loop Only of next 17 sts, work FPdc around each of next 6 FPdc, sc in Back Loop Only of next 6 sts, work FPdc around each of next 4 FPdc, sc in Back Loop Only of next 3 sts, work FPdc around each of next 2 FPdc, sc in Back Loop Only of next 6 sc, work FPdc around each of next 17 FPdc, sc in Back Loop Only of next 8 sts, work FPdc around each of next 18 FPdc, sc in Back Loop Only of each st across to next ch-1 sp, (hdc, ch 1, hdc) in next ch-1 sp, sc in Back Loop Only of next 15 sts, dc in free loop of next sc on Rnd 49, work FPdc around next dc, sc in Back Loop Only of next sc, work FPdc around next FPdc, sc in Back Loop Only of next 6 sc, work FPdc around next FPdc, sc in Back Loop Only of next sc, work FPdc around each of next 2 sts, sc in Back Loop Only of next 12 sts, work FPdc around each of next 14 FPdc, sc in Back Loop Only of next 17 sts, work FPdc around each of next 12 sts, dc in free loop of next FPdc on Rnd 49, work FPdc around next FPdc, sc in Back Loop Only of each st across to next ch-1 sp †, (hdc, ch 1, hdc) in next ch-1 sp; repeat from † to † once, hdc in same sp as first hdc, sc in first hdc to form last ch-1 sp: 420 sts and 4 ch-1 sps.

Rnd 52: Ch 2, † sc in Back Loop Only of next 18 sts, work FPdc around each of next 5 FPdc, sc in Back Loop Only of next 8 sts, work FPdc around each of next 3 FPdc, sc in Back Loop only of next 3 sc, work FPdc around each of next 2 FPdc, sc in Back Loop Only of next 6 sc, work FPdc around each of next 5 FPdc, sc in Back Loop Only of next 3 FPdc, work FPdc around each of next 8 FPdc, sc in Back Loop Only of next 8 sts, dc in free loop of next sc on Rnd 50, sc in Back Loop Only of next FPdc, work FPdc around each of next 4 FPdc, sc in Back Loop Only of next 7 FPdc, work FPdc around each of next 6 FPdc, sc in Back Loop Only of each st across to next ch-1 sp, (hdc, ch 1, hdc) in next ch-1 sp, sc in Back Loop Only of next 16 sts, work FPdc around next dc, sc in Back Loop Only of next 2 sts, work FPdc around next FPdc, sc in Back Loop Only of next 6 sc, work FPdc around next FPdc, sc in Back Loop Only of next 2 sts, work FPdc around next FPdc, sc in Back Loop Only of next 12 sc, work FPdc around each of next 6 FPdc, sc in Back Loop Only of next 2 FPdc, work FPdc around each of next 6 FPdc, sc in Back Loop Only of next 15 sc, dc in free loop of next 2 sc on Rnd 50, work FPdc around each of next 4 FPdc, sc in Back Loop Only of next 3 FPdc, work FPdc around each of next 6 sts, sc in Back Loop Only of each st across to next ch-1 sp †, (hdc, ch 1, hdc) in next ch-1 sp; repeat from † to † once, hdc in same sp as first hdc, sc in first hdc to form last ch-1 sp: 428 sts and 4 ch-1 sps.

Instructions continued on page 40.

Rnd 53: Ch 2, † sc in Back Loop Only of next 19 sts, work FPdc around each of next 5 FPdc, sc in Back Loop Only of next 8 sc, work FPdc around each of next 3 FPdc, sc in Back Loop Only of next 3 sc, work FPdc around each of next 2 FPdc, sc in Back Loop Only of next 5 sc, dc in free loop of next sc on Rnd 51, work FPdc around each of next 4 FPdc, sc in Back Loop Only of next 6 sts, work FPdc around each of next 5 FPdc, sc in Back Loop Only of next 9 sts, work FPdc around next dc, sc in Back Loop Only of next sc, work FPdc around each of next 4 FPdc, sc in Back Loop Only of next 7 sc, work FPdc around each of next 4 FPdc, sc in Back Loop Only of each st across to next ch-1 sp, (hdc, ch 1, hdc) in next ch-1 sp, sc in Back Loop Only of next 17 sts, work FPdc around next FPdc, sc in Back Loop Only of next 2 sc, work FPdc around next FPdc, dc in free loop of next sc on Rnd 51, sc in Back Loop Only of next 5 sc, work FPdc around next FPdc, sc in Back Loop Only of next 2 sc, work FPdc around next FPdc, sc in Back Loop Only of next 12 sc, work FPdc around each of next 4 FPdc, sc in Back Loop Only of next 5 sts, work FPdc around each of next 4 FPdc, sc in Back Loop Only of next 16 sts, work FPdc around each of next 5 sts, sc in Back Loop Only of next 7 sts, work FPdc around each of next 3 FPdc, dc in free loop of next st on Rnd 51, sc in Back Loop Only of each st across to next ch-1 sp †, (hdc, ch 1, hdc) in next ch-1 sp; repeat from † to † once, hdc in same sp as first hdc, sc in first hdc to form last ch-1 sp: 436 sts and 4 ch-1 sps.

Rnd 54: Ch 2, † sc in Back Loop Only of next 21 sts, work FPdc around each of next 4 FPdc, sc in Back Loop Only of next 8 sc, work FPdc around each of next 3 FPdc, sc in Back Loop Only of next sc, dc in free loop of next 2 sc on Rnd 52, work FPdc around next FPdc, sc in Back Loop Only of next 6 sts, work FPdc around each of next 4 sts, sc in Back Loop Only of next 7 sts, work FPdc around each of next 2 FPdc, sc in Back Loop Only of next FPdc, work FPdc around each of next 2 FPdc, dc in free loop of next dc on Rnd 52, sc in Back Loop Only of next 10 sts, work FPdc around each of next 4 FPdc, sc in Back Loop Only of next 8 sts, work FPdc around each of next 3 FPdc, sc in Back Loop Only of each st across to next ch-1 sp, (hdc, ch 1, hdc) in next ch-1 sp, sc in Back Loop Only of next 18 sts, work FPdc around next FPdc, sc in Back Loop Only of next 3 sts, work FPdc around next dc, sc in Back Loop Only of next 5 sc,

work FPdc around next FPdc, sc in Back Loop Only of next 2 sc, work FPdc around next FPdc, sc in Back Loop Only of next 12 sc, work FPdc around each of next 3 FPdc, sc in Back Loop Only of next 6 sts, work FPdc around each of next 4 FPdc, sc in Back Loop Only of next 16 sc, work FPdc around each of next 4 sts, sc in Back Loop Only of next 8 sts, work FPdc around each of next 4 sts, dc in free loop of next sc on Rnd 52, sc in Back Loop Only of each st across to next ch-1 sp †, (hdc, ch 1, hdc) in next ch-1 sp; repeat from † to † once, hdc in same sp as first hdc, sc in first hdc to form last ch-1 sp: 444 sts and 4 ch-1 sps.

Rnd 55: Ch 2, † sc in Back Loop Only of next 22 sts, work FPdc around each of next 4 FPdc, sc in Back Loop Only of next 8 sc, work FPdc around each of next 3 FPdc, sc in Back Loop Only of next 2 sts, work FPdc around next dc, sc in Back Loop Only of next 7 sts, work FPdc around each of next 2 FPdc, sc in Back Loop Only of next FPdc, work FPdc around next FPdc, dc in free loop of next dc on Rnd 53, sc in Back Loop Only of next 6 sc, work FPdc around each of next 2 FPdc, sc in Back Loop Only of next 3 sts, work FPdc around next dc, dc in free loop of next sc on Rnd 53, sc in Back Loop Only of next 9 sc, work FPdc around each of next 4 FPdc, dc in free loop of next sc on Rnd 53, sc in Back Loop Only of next 7 sc, work FPdc around each of next 3 FPdc, dc in free loop of next sc on Rnd 53, sc in Back Loop Only of each st across to next ch-1 sp, (hdc, ch 1, hdc) in next ch-1 sp, sc in Back Loop Only of next 19 sts, work FPdc around next FPdc, sc in Back Loop Only of next 3 sc, work FPdc around next FPdc, sc in Back Loop Only of next 5 sc, work FPdc around next FPdc, sc in Back Loop Only of next 3 sts, dc in free loop of next sc on Rnd 53, sc in Back Loop Only of next 11 sc, work FPdc around each of next 3 FPdc, dc in free loop of next FPdc on Rnd 53, sc in Back Loop Only of next 5 sc, work FPdc around each of next 4 FPdc, sc in Back Loop Only of next 16 sc, work FPdc around each of next 2 FPdc, sc in Back Loop Only of next FPdc, work FPdc around next FPdc, dc in free loop of next FPdc on Rnd 53, sc in Back Loop Only of next 7 sc, work FPdc around each of next 2 FPdc, sc in Back Loop Only of next 2 FPdc, work FPdc around next dc, dc in free loop of next sc on Rnd 53, sc in Back Loop Only of each st across to next ch-1 sp †, (hdc, ch 1, hdc) in next ch-1 sp; repeat from † to † once, hdc in same sp as first hdc, sc in first hdc to form last ch-1 sp: 452 sts and 4 ch-1 sps.

Rnd 56: Ch 2, † sc in Back Loop Only of next 23 sts, work FPdc around each of next 4 FPdc, sc in Back Loop Only of next 8 sc, work FPdc around each of next 3 FPdc, sc in Back Loop Only of next 11 sts, work FPdc around next FPdc, dc in free loop of next FPdc on Rnd 54, sc in Back Loop Only of next FPdc, work FPdc around next dc, dc in free loop of next sc on Rnd 54, sc in Back Loop Only of next 6 sts, work FPdc around next FPdc, dc in free loop of next sc on Rnd 54, sc in Back Loop Only of next 3 sts, work FPdc around next st, dc in free loop of next sc on Rnd 54, sc in Back Loop Only of next 9 sts, work FPdc around each of next 4 sts, sc in Back Loop Only of next 9 sts, work FPdc around each of next 2 sts, dc in free loop of next sc on Rnd 54, sc in Back Loop Only of each st across to next ch-1 sp, (hdc, ch 1, hdc) in next ch-1 sp, sc in Back Loop Only of next 20 sts, work FPdc around next FPdc, dc in free loop of next sc on Rnd 54, sc in Back Loop Only of next 3 sts, dc in free loop of next 2 sc on Rnd 54, sc in Back Loop Only of next 3 sc, work FPdc around next FPdc, dc in free loop of next sc on Rnd 54, sc in Back Loop Only of next 2 sc, work FPdc around next dc, dc in free loop of next sc on Rnd 54, sc in Back Loop Only of next 11 sts, work FPdc around each of next 3 sts, dc in free loop of next sc on Rnd 54, sc in Back Loop Only of next 5 sts, work FPdc around each of next 3 FPdc, dc in free loop of next sc on Rnd 54, sc in Back Loop Only of next 16 sts, work FPdc around next FPdc, dc in free loop of next FPdc on Rnd 54, sc in Back Loop Only of next FPdc, work FPdc around next FPdc, dc in free loop of next sc on Rnd 54, sc in Back Loop Only of next 7 sts, work FPdc around next FPdc, dc in free loop of next FPdc on Rnd 54, sc in Back Loop Only of next 2 sts, work FPdc around next dc, dc in free loop of next sc on Rnd 54, sc in Back Loop Only of each st across to next ch-1 sp †, (hdc, ch 1, hdc) in next ch-1 sp; repeat from † to † once, hdc in same sp as first hdc, sc in first hdc to form last ch-1 sp: 460 sts and 4 ch-1 sps.

Rnds 57 and 58: Ch 2, ★ † sc in Back Loop Only of each st across to next ch-1 sp †, (hdc, ch 1, hdc) in next ch-1 sp; repeat from ★ 2 times **more**, then repeat from † to † once, hdc in same sp as first hdc, sc in first hdc to form last ch-1 sp: 476 sts and 4 ch-1 sps.

Rnd 59: Ch 2, ★ † hdc in Back Loop Only of next hdc, (ch 1, skip next sc, hdc in Back Loop Only of next st) across to next ch-1 sp †, (hdc, ch 1, hdc) in next ch-1 sp; repeat from ★ 2 times **more**, then repeat from † to † once, hdc in same sp as first hdc, sc in first hdc to form last ch-1 sp: 248 hdc and 240 ch-1 sps.

Rnd 60: Ch 2, ★ † skip next hdc, hdc in Back Loop Only of next hdc and each hdc and each ch across to next corner ch-1 sp †, (hdc, ch 1, hdc) in corner ch-1 sp; repeat from ★ 2 times **more**, then repeat from † to † once, hdc in same sp as first hdc, sc in first hdc to form last ch-1 sp: 488 hdc and 4 ch-1 sps.

Rnd 61: Ch 2, ★ † sc in Back Loop Only of next 2 hdc, (work FPdc around each of next 2 hdc, sc in Back Loop Only of next 2 hdc) across to next ch-1 sp †, (hdc, ch 1, hdc) in next ch-1 sp; repeat from ★ 2 times **more**, then repeat from † to † once, hdc in same sp as first hdc, sc in first hdc to form last ch-1 sp: 496 sts and 4 ch-1 sps.

Rnd 62: Ch 2, ★ † work FPdc around next hdc, sc in Back Loop Only of next 2 sc, (work FPdc around each of next 2 FPdc, sc in Back Loop Only of next 2 sc) across to within one st of next ch-1 sp, work FPdc around next hdc †, (hdc, ch 1, hdc) in next ch-1 sp; repeat from ★ 2 times **more**, then repeat from † to † once, hdc in same sp as first hdc, sc in first hdc to form last ch-1 sp: 504 sts and 4 ch-1 sps.

Rnd 63: Ch 2, ★ † work FPdc around each of next 2 sts, (sc in Back Loop Only of next 2 sc, work FPdc around each of next 2 sts) across to next ch-1 sp †, (hdc, ch 1, hdc) in next ch-1 sp; repeat from ★ 2 times **more**, then repeat from † to † once, hdc in same sp as first hdc, ch 1, join with slip st to first hdc: 512 sts and 4 ch-1 sps.

Rnd 64: Ch 1, sc in same st and in each st across to next ch-1 sp, (sc, hdc, dc, hdc, sc) in next ch-1 sp, ★ sc in each st across to next ch-1 sp, (sc, hdc, dc, hdc, sc) in next ch-1 sp; repeat from ★ 2 times **more**; join with slip st to first sc, finish off.

PLACEMENT DIAGRAM

1	2	3	4	5	6	7	8	9	10	11	12
2	3	4	5	6	7	8	9	10	11	12	1
3	4	5	6	7	8	9	10	11	12	1	2
4	5	6	7	8	9	10	11	12	1	2	3
5	6	7	8	9	10	11	12	1	2	3	4
6	7	8	9	10	11	12	1	2	3	4	5
7	8	9	10	11	12	1	2	3	4	5	6
8	9	10	11	12	1	2	3	4	5	6	7
9	10	11	12	1	2	3	4	5	6	7	8
10	11	12	1	2	3	4	5	6	7	8	9
11	12	1	2	3	4	5	6	7	8	9	10
12	1	2	3	4	5	6	7	8	9	10	11
1	2	3	4	5	6	7	8	9	10	11	12
2	3	4	5	6	7	8	9	10	11	12	1
3	4	5	6	7	8	9	10	11	12	1	2

EDGING

Rnd 1: With **right** side facing, join White with slip st in first corner ch-1 sp; ch 1, sc in same sp, ch 3, ★ † skip next dc, (sc in next st, ch 3, skip next st) 6 times, [sc in next joining, ch 3, skip next dc, (sc in next st, ch 3, skip next st) 6 times] across to next corner ch-1 sp †, (sc, ch 3) twice in corner ch-1 sp; repeat from ★ 2 times **more**, then repeat from † to † once, sc in same sp as first sc, ch 3; join with slip st to first sc: 382 sc and 382 ch-3 sps.

Rnd 2: Slip st in first ch-3 sp, ch 1, 2 sc in same sp, 3 sc in next ch-3 sp and in each ch-3 sp around, sc in same sp as first sc; join with slip st to first sc: 1,146 sc.

Rnd 3: Ch 3, 2 dc in same st, ★ skip next 2 sc, (3 dc in next sc, skip next 2 sc) across to center sc of next corner 3-sc group, 6 dc in center sc; repeat from ★ 3 times **more**; join with slip st to first dc: 378 3-dc groups and 4 6-dc groups.

Rnd 4: Ch 4, skip next 2 dc, [slip st in sp **before** next dc *(Fig. 6a, page 46)*, ch 4, skip next 3 dc] around, slip st in same st as previous joining; finish off.

Row 8: With **right** side facing, join Pink with sc in first dc; sc in next 7 dc, working in **front** of previous rows, dtr in second skipped sc 3 rows **below**, skip dc **behind** dtr on previous row, sc in next 2 dc, working in **front** of last dtr made, dtr in first skipped sc 3 rows **below**, ★ skip dc **behind** dtr on previous row, sc in next 4 dc, skip next skipped sc 3 rows **below**, working in **front** of previous rows, dtr in next skipped sc, skip dc **behind** dtr on previous row, sc in next 2 dc, working in **front** of last dtr made, dtr in skipped sc 3 rows **below**; repeat from ★ across to last 9 dc, skip dc **behind** dtr on previous row, sc in last 8 dc; finish off: 138 sc and 42 dtr.

Row 9: With **wrong** side facing, join Pink with sc in first sc; sc in next sc and in each st across; finish off: 180 sc.

Rows 10-125: Repeat Rows 2-9, 14 times; then repeat Rows 2-5 once **more**.

TRIM
FIRST SIDE

With **right** side facing, join Pink with sc in first sc on Row 125; sc in next sc and in each sc across; finish off.

SECOND SIDE

With **right** side facing and working in free loops of beginning ch *(Fig. 4b, page 45)*, join Pink with sc in first ch; sc in next ch and in each ch across; finish off.

Using one 16" (40.5 cm) strand of corresponding color yarn for each fringe, add fringe across short edges of Afghan *(Figs. 8a & b, page 46)*.

Row 7: With **right** side facing, join Brown with slip st in first dc; ch 3, dc in sp **before** next dc, ch 1, (skip next 3 sts, 2 dc in sp **before** next dc, ch 1) across to last 4 sts, skip next 3 sts, dc in sp **before** next dc, dc in last dc: 66 dc and 32 ch-1 sps.

Row 8: Ch 3, turn; dc in sp **before** next dc, ch 1, (skip next 2 dc, 2 dc in sp **before** next dc, ch 1) across to last 3 dc, skip next 2 dc, dc in sp **before** next dc, dc in last dc changing to Ecru.

Rows 9-69: Repeat Rows 3-8, 10 times; then repeat Row 3 once **more**. Do **not** finish off at end of Row 69.

EDGING

Rnd 1: Using smaller size hook, ch 1, do **not** turn; working in end of rows, work 137 sc evenly spaced across; working in free loops of beginning ch *(Fig. 4b, page 45)*, (sc, ch 2, sc) in first ch, work 95 sc evenly spaced across to marked ch, (sc, ch 2, sc) in marked ch; working in end of rows, work 137 sc evenly spaced across; working in sts across Row 69, (sc, ch 2, sc) in first dc, skip next dc, sc next st and in each st across to last dc, (sc, ch 2, sc) in last dc; join with slip st to first sc, finish off: 472 sc and 4 ch-2 sps.

Rnd 2: With **right** side facing, join Brown with slip st in any corner ch-2 sp; ch 1, (sc, ch 2, sc) in same sp, ★ ch 1, skip next sc, (sc in next sc, ch 1, skip next sc) across to next corner ch-2 sp, (sc, ch 2, sc) in corner ch-2 sp; repeat from ★ 2 times **more**, ch 1, skip next sc, (sc in next sc, ch 1, skip next sc) across; join with slip st to first sc, finish off: 242 sps.

Rnd 3: With **right** side facing, join Ecru with slip st in any corner ch-2 sp; ch 1, (sc, ch 2, sc) in same sp, ★ ch 1, (sc in next ch-1 sp, ch 1) across to next corner ch-2 sp, (sc, ch 2, sc) in corner ch-2 sp; repeat from ★ 2 times **more**, ch 1, (sc in next ch-1 sp, ch 1) across; join with slip st to first sc, do **not** finish off: 246 sps.

Rnd 4: Slip st in first ch-2 sp, ch 6 (**counts as first dc plus ch 3**), dc in same sp, ★ 2 dc in each ch-1 sp across to next corner ch-2 sp, (dc, ch 3, dc) in corner ch-2 sp; repeat from ★ 2 times **more**, 2 dc in each ch-1 sp across; join with slip st to first dc: 492 dc and 4 ch-2 sps.

Rnd 5: Slip st in first ch-3 sp, ch 1, sc in same sp, ch 3, ★ (sc in next dc, ch 3, skip next dc) across to next corner ch-3 sp, sc in corner ch-3 sp, ch 3; repeat from ★ 2 times **more**, (sc in next dc, ch 3, skip next dc) across; join with slip st to first sc; finish off.

Rnds 3 and 4: Ch 1, sc in last ch-5 sp made, ch 5, ★ (sc in next ch-5 sp, ch 5) across to next corner ch-5 sp, (sc, ch 5) twice in corner ch-5 sp; repeat from ★ 2 times **more**, (sc in next ch-5 sp, ch 5) across, sc in same sp as first sc, ch 2, dc in first sc to form last ch-5 sp: 188 ch-5 sps.

Rnd 5: Ch 1, (sc, ch 5) twice in last ch-5 sp made, ★ (sc in next ch-5 sp, ch 5) across to next corner ch-5 sp, (sc, ch 5) twice in corner ch-5 sp; repeat from ★ 2 times **more**, (sc in next ch-5 sp, ch 5) across; join with slip st to first sc, finish off.

Optional: Beginning and ending in same corner and leaving a 12" (30.5 cm) length, weave ribbon through Eyelet Rnd. Tie in bow and trim ends.

General Instructions

Abbreviations

ch(s)	chain(s)
cm	centimeters
dc	double crochet(s)
dtr	double treble crochet(s)
FPdc	Front Post double crochet(s)
hdc	half double crochet(s)
LDC	Long Double Crochet(s)
LTR	Long Treble Crochet(s)
mm	millimeters
Rnd(s)	Round(s)
sc	single crochet(s)
sp(s)	space(s)
st(s)	stitch(es)
tr	treble crochet(s)
YO	yarn over

★ — work instructions following ★ as **many more** times as indicated in addition to the first time.

† to † — work all instructions from first † to second † as **many** times as specified.

( ) or [ ] — work enclosed instructions **as many** times as specified by the number immediately following **or** work all enclosed instructions in the stitch or space indicated **or** contains explanatory remarks.

colon (:) — the number(s) given after a colon at the end of a row or round denote(s) the number of stitches and/or spaces you should have on that row or round.

Yarn Weight Symbol & Names	LACE 0	SUPER FINE 1	FINE 2	LIGHT 3	MEDIUM 4	BULKY 5	SUPER BULKY 6
Type of Yarns in Category	Fingering, 10-count crochet thread	Sock, Fingering Baby	Sport, Baby	DK, Light Worsted	Worsted, Afghan, Aran	Chunky, Craft, Rug	Bulky, Roving
Crochet Gauge* Ranges in Single Crochet to 4" (10 cm)	32-42 double crochets**	21-32 sts	16-20 sts	12-17 sts	11-14 sts	8-11 sts	5-9 sts
Advised Hook Size Range	Steel*** 6,7,8 Regular hook B-1	B-1 to E-4	E-4 to 7	7 to I-9	I-9 to K-10.5	K-10.5 to M-13	M-13 and larger

*GUIDELINES ONLY: The chart above reflects the most commonly used gauges and hook sizes for specific yarn categories.

** Lace weight yarns are usually crocheted on larger-size hooks to create lacy openwork patterns. Accordingly, a gauge range is difficult to determine. Always follow the gauge stated in your pattern.

CROCHET TERMINOLOGY

UNITED STATES		INTERNATIONAL
slip stitch (slip st)	=	single crochet (sc)
single crochet (sc)	=	double crochet (dc)
half double crochet (hdc)	=	half treble crochet (htr)
double crochet (dc)	=	treble crochet (tr)
treble crochet (tr)	=	double treble crochet (dtr)
double treble crochet (dtr)	=	triple treble crochet (ttr)
triple treble crochet (tr tr)	=	quadruple treble crochet (qtr)
skip	=	miss

CROCHET HOOKS

U.S.	B-1	C-2	D-3	E-4	F-5	G-6	H-8	I-9	J-10	K-10½	N	P	Q
Metric - mm	2.25	2.75	3.25	3.5	3.75	4	5	5.5	6	6.5	9	10	15

■□□□ BEGINNER	Projects for first-time crocheters using basic stitches. Minimal shaping.
■■□□ EASY	Projects using yarn with basic stitches, repetitive stitch patterns, simple color changes, and simple shaping and finishing.
■■■□ INTERMEDIATE	Projects using a variety of techniques, such as basic lace patterns or color patterns, mid-level shaping and finishing.
■■■■ EXPERIENCED	Projects with intricate stitch patterns, techniques and dimension, such as non-repeating patterns, multi-color techniques, fine threads, small hooks, detailed shaping and refined finishing.

Gauge

Exact gauge is **essential** for proper size. Before beginning your Afghan, make the sample swatch given in the individual instructions in the yarn and hook specified. After completing the swatch, measure it, counting your stitches and rows or rounds carefully. If your swatch is larger or smaller than specified, **make another, changing hook size to get the correct gauge.** Keep trying until you find the size hook that will give you the specified gauge.

Joining With Sc

When instructed to join with sc, begin with a slip knot on hook. Insert hook in stitch or space indicated, YO and pull up a loop, YO and draw through both loops on hook.

Joining With Dc

When instructed to join with dc, begin with a slip knot on hook. YO, holding loop on hook, insert hook in stitch or space indicated, YO and pull up a loop (3 loops on hook), (YO and draw through 2 loops on hook) twice.

Back Loop Only

Work only in loop(s) indicated by arrow *(Fig. 1)*.

Fig. 1

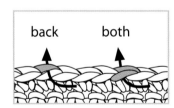

Working In Front Of, Around, Or Behind A Stitch

Work in stitch or space indicated, inserting hook in direction of arrow *(Fig. 2)*.

Fig. 2

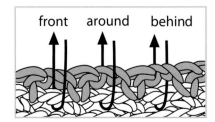

Back Ridge

Work only in loops indicated by arrows *(Fig. 3)*.

Fig. 3

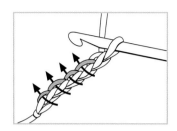

Free Loops

After working in Back or Front Loops Only on a row or round, there will be a ridge of unused loops. These are called the free loops. Later, when instructed to work in the free loops of the same row or round, work in these loops *(Fig. 4a)*. When instructed to work in free loops of a chain, work in loop indicated by arrow *(Fig. 4b)*.

Fig. 4a   **Fig. 4b**

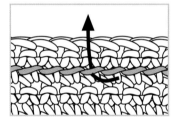 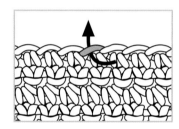

Post Stitch

Work around post of stitch indicated, inserting hook in direction of arrow *(Fig. 5)*.

Fig. 5

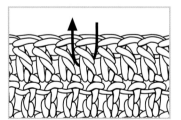

Working In Space Before A Stitch

When instructed to work in space before a stitch, insert hook in space indicated by arrow *(Figs. 6a & b)*.

Fig. 6a

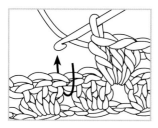

Fig. 6b

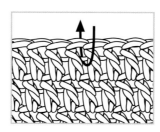

Whipstitch

Place two Squares or Strips with wrong sides together. Sew through both pieces once to secure the beginning of the seam, leaving an ample yarn end to weave in later. Insert the needle from front to back through inside loops on both pieces *(Fig. 7a)* or through both loops on both pieces *(Fig. 7b)*. Bring the needle around and insert it from front to back through next loops of both pieces. Continue in this manner across.

Fig. 7a

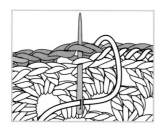

Fig. 7b

Fringe

Cut a piece of cardboard 3" (7.5 cm) wide and half as long as strands indicated in individual instructions. Wind the yarn loosely and evenly lengthwise around the cardboard until the card is filled, then cut across one end; repeat as needed.

Hold together as many strands as specified in individual instructions; fold in half.

With wrong side facing and using a crochet hook, draw the folded end up through a row and pull the loose ends through the folded end *(Fig. 8a)*; draw the knot up tightly *(Fig. 8b)*. Repeat, spacing as specified in individual instructions.

Lay flat on a hard surface and trim the ends.

Fig. 8a

Fig. 8b

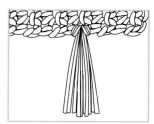

Yarn Information

The afghans in this leaflet were made using various weights of yarn. Any brand of the specified weight of yarn may be used. It is best to refer to the yardage/meters when determining how many balls or skeins to purchase. Remember, to arrive at the finished size, it is the GAUGE/TENSION that is important, not the brand of yarn. For your convenience, listed below are the specific yarns used to create our photography models.

JANUARY
Patons® Canadiana
White - #1 White
Lt Blue - #29 Lt Blue
Blue - #302 Faded Denim
Dk Blue - #303 Denim

FEBRUARY
Caron® Cuddlesoft
#2747 Baby Lavender
Note: We regret any inconvenience, but this yarn has been discontinued.

MARCH
Bernat® Softee® Baby
White - #2000 White
Green - #2004 Mint
Yellow - #2003 Lemon

APRIL
Red Heart® Super Saver®
Blue - #0381 Lt Blue
Variegated - #345 Baby Print

MAY
TLC® Baby
#5737 Powder Pink

JUNE
Caron® Cuddlesoft
#2746 Baby Turquoise
Note: We regret any inconvenience, but this yarn has been discontinued.

JULY
Lion Brand® Microspun
White - #100 Lily White
Blue - #144 Lilac
Red - #113 Cherry Red

AUGUST
Caron® Wintuk®
#3026 Baby Blue

SEPTEMBER
Moda Dea® Baby Talk™
White - #7201 White
Blue - #7281 Baby Blue
Pink - #7235 Lt Pink
Green - #7253 Kiwi
Orange - #7257 Orange
Yellow - #7230 Lemon Yellow
Lavender - #7236 Lilac

OCTOBER
Patons® Astra
White - #2751 White
Pink - #2752 Baby Pink

NOVEMBER
Lion Brand® Cotton-Ease
Ecru - #099 Almond
Brown - #122 Taupe
Gold - #186 Maize

DECEMBER
Red Heart® Super Saver®
#311 White

Production Team

Instructional Editor
Katie Galucki

Technical Editor
Cathy Hardy

Contributing Technical Editor
Valesha M. Kirksey

Senior Graphic Artist
Lora Puls

Graphic Artist
Jeanne Zaffarano

Photo Stylist
Christy Meyers

Photographer
Ken West

Items made and instructions tested by Susan Carter, Marianna Crowder and Dale Potter.

Discover the creative world of Leisure Arts Publications, Where Inspiration Lives on Every Page.

This one's for you, baby...

You'll go Ga-Ga over these "how to" crochet baby fashions.

#4056

#3861

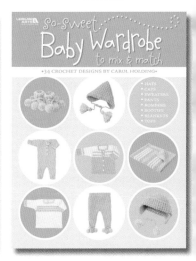

#3666

#4339

Visit your favorite retailer, or shop online at leisurearts.com. For more inspiration, sign up for our free e-newsletter and receive free projects, reviews of our newest books, handy tips, and more.